FALLEN
...AND SPIRITS OF THE DARK
ANGELS

FALLEN
...AND SPIRITS OF THE DARK
ANGELS

ROBERT MASELLO

A Perigee Book

A Perigee Book
Published by The Berkley Publishing Group
200 Madison Avenue
New York, NY 10016

Copyright © 1994 by Robert Masello

Book design by Joseph Perez

Cover design by Keith Sheridan Associates, Inc.

Cover engraving by Gustave Doré

First edition: October 1994

Published simultaneously in Canada.

Library of Congress Cataloging-in-Publication Data
Masello, Robert.
        Fallen angels : and spirits of the dark / by
    Robert Masello. — 1st Perigee ed.
                p.   cm.
        "A Perigee book"—T.p. verso.
        Includes bibliographical references.
        ISBN 0-399-51889-4 (paper : acid-free paper)
        1. Demonology.   2. Witchcraft   3. Vampires   4. Occultism.
    I. Title
    BF1531.M33   1994   94-16797
    133.4'2—dc20   CIP

Printed in the United States of America

10   9   8   7   6   5   4   3   2   1

This book is printed on acid-free paper.

For a trio of English teachers—
Ronald Gearring, Curtis Crotty,
      and Barbara Pannwitt—
who put me through basic training
at Evanston Township High School

CONTENTS

"The fiend with all his comrades
Fell then from heaven above,
Through as long as three nights and days,
The angels from heaven into hell;
And them all the Lord transformed to devils,
Because they his deed and word
Would not revere."

Caedmon, *Creation: The Fall of the Rebel Angels* (c. A.D. 670)

PREFACE

*E*ver since the first night fell, ever since men and women first clustered around their primitive fires and learned to speak, there have been stories — stories meant to allay our common fears, stories meant to bring order to a chaotic world, stories meant to explain our place on Earth and in the cosmos.

One of the most timeless of these stories is that of Lucifer, a great angel who once challenged the rule of God and, for his terrible presumption, was cast down from Heaven. From that time forward, according to the Scriptures, Lucifer and his cohorts —fallen angels all — have bent their evil will to the spreading of mayhem, death, and destruction in the world.

The occult world that they inhabit — the mysterious home of dark forces and unseen creatures — has found many eager tenants: demons who work to corrupt mankind, ghouls who feed on corruption, witches who do the Devil's bidding, ghosts who forever enact an ancient misery.

And the night has spawned a fearful brood of its own — vampires who drain the blood of the living, werewolves who devour the flesh, imps and spirits who haunt the dreams and bedchambers of unsuspecting mortals.

The unholy roll call is a long one, but here assembled are some of its most terrifying soldiers, the supernatural creatures and their all-too-willing human recruits. It may not be a world you would wish to live in, but it may be one you would like to know. As the old saying goes, fore-warned is forearmed. And against invisible enemies, most of all, it may be wise to have all the warning, and protection, you can get . . . .

SATAN AND HIS COURT

"........ *H*ail horrours, hail
Infernal world, and thou profoundest Hell
Receive thy new Possessor; One who brings
A mind not to be chang'd by Place or Time.
The mind is its own place, and in it self
Can make a Heav'n of Hell, a Hell of Heav'n.
What matter where, if I be still the same,
And what should I be, all but less than he
Whom thunder hath made greater? Here at least
We shall be free; th' Almighty hath not built
Here for his envy, will not drive us hence:
Here we may reign secure, and in my choyce
To reign is worth ambition though in Hell:
Better to reign in Hell, than serve in Heav'n."

John Milton, *Paradise Lost*
(Book I)

BRIGHT ANGEL

*I*n Heaven, his name was **Lucifer** ("light bearer"), and he was God's most beautiful angel. But even with such an enviable position, Lucifer wasn't content. He took inordinate pride in his own angelic nature — he was pleased with his supernatural gifts, his immortality, his closeness to God. And eventually, his pride became so great that he chafed at having a master at all, even God. He wanted to control his own destiny, and so he rebelled. He threw up his banner, recruited an army of equally discontented angels, and waged war for supremacy.

To lead His own troops into battle, God appointed the archangel Michael his field commander:

> "And there was war in heaven: Michael and his angels
> fought against the dragon; and the dragon fought and his
> angels, and prevailed not; neither was their place found
> any more in heaven. And the great dragon was cast out,
> that old serpent, called the Devil, and Satan, which

deceiveth the whole world; he was cast out into the earth, and his angels were cast out with him . . . Therefore rejoice, ye heavens, and ye that dwell in them. Woe to the inhabiters of the earth and of the sea! for the devil is come down unto you, having great wrath . . ."

(Revelation 12: 7–9, 12)

Having fallen from Heaven, Lucifer was no more — now he had a new name, Satan (the Hebrew word for "adversary"), and his new dominion was Hell. The angels who had fallen with him (as determined by the Fourth Lateran Council in A.D. 1215) were his demons. Accursed by God, doomed to eternal torment themselves, Satan and company found a new vocation in the temptation and corruption of man. With nothing better to occupy their time, they resolved to take out their "great wrath" on mortals too foolish or sinful to resist their lures.

As the world's sad history will attest, there was never any shortage of such mortals.

THE WATCHERS

𝒯here is another story, one that is hinted at in the first book of the Bible, to account for Lucifer's legions. According to this story, which is more fully recounted in 1 Enoch (a Hebrew book that did not find its way into the Old Testament), there was once an order of angels known as the Watchers. As their name might suggest, the Watchers kept a close eye on the affairs of men — too close an eye, as it turns out.

It seems that staying up all night (the Watchers never slept) and studying the newly minted females of the human race gave them some bad ideas. "And it came to pass, when men began to multiply on the face of the earth, and daughters were born unto them, that the Sons of God saw the daughters of men that they were fair; and they took them wives of all which they chose." (Genesis 6:1–2.) The Watchers not only came down to earth and mated — they also instructed their wives in all sorts of forbidden and arcane arts. They taught them botany, astrology, and astronomy. They showed them how to make magic and weapons, and, surprisingly, how to use cosmetics. God was not pleased.

And His displeasure increased when the offspring of these angels were born. These young ones turned out not to be angels, but monsters —

great giants who killed and ate any unlucky humans whom they caught. And if there weren't any humans around, they satisfied their huge appetites by killing and devouring one another. Clearly, this was not what God had had in mind for the Earth, and once again he enlisted Michael to help him with straightening things out. God wiped out the giants, while Michael rounded up the fallen angels and imprisoned them in the valleys of the Earth where they would stay until the time came for them to be hurled into the everlasting fire. According to this account, stitched together from Genesis and Enoch, it is these under-ground angels—these Watchers who would watch no more—who comprised Lucifer's rebel army.

SON OF THE MORNING

$\mathcal{F}$or yet another view of Lucifer's fall, one that takes what might safely be described as a gloating tone, here's Isaiah 14:12–17:

> "How art thou fallen from heaven, O Lucifer, son of the morning! how art thou cut down to the ground, which didst weaken the nations! For thou hast said in thine heart, I will ascend into heaven, I will exalt my throne above the stars of God: I will sit also upon the mount of the

Asmodeus, a demon of fury and lust.

congregation, in the sides of the north: I will ascend above the heights of the clouds; I will be like the Most High. Yet thou shalt be brought down to hell, to the sides of the pit. They that see thee shall narrowly look upon thee, and consider thee, saying, Is this the man that made the earth to tremble, that did shake kingdoms; that made the world as a wilderness, and destroyed the cities thereof . . . ?"

But how, you may ask, did Lucifer come to be referred to as "son of the morning"? In part, it was because his name, Lucifer, was the name the Romans had given to the morning star, the last star each day to be obscured by the rising sun. And partly it was because in at least one ancient myth, of Hebrew origins, this same morning star had tried to outblaze the sun itself, but had, of course, been vanquished in the end. The close analogy to Lucifer, the bright angel who had in his pride thought to displace God Himself and been brought down because of it, isn't hard to see.

"MY NAME IS LEGION"

In Mark 5:2 through 5:9, we are told that when Jesus disembarked in the land of the Gadarenes, He encountered a man possessed by demons, "a man with an unclean spirit, who had his dwelling among the tombs . . . and always, night and day, he was in the mountains, and in the tombs, crying, and cutting himself with stones." When the man accosted Jesus, Jesus spoke to the demon who possessed him and said, "Come out of the man, thou unclean spirit. And he asked him, What is thy name? And he answered, saying, My name is Legion: for we are many."

So how many demons are there? What are their proper names? And what specific powers do they possess? Even Jesus couldn't get a very clear answer — and priests, theologians, and demonologists have been debating the same questions ever since.

When St. Macarius of Alexandria begged the Lord to let him see the hosts of evil, the Lord obliged — and Macarius claims they were "as numerous as bees." Still not very specific. In 1459 Alphonsus de Spina took a more mathematical approach. He estimated that roughly one-third of the original angels had rebelled and become, as a result, demons: that number, he declared, came to 133,306,608. But other experts begged to differ. One claimed that there were 66 princes in Hell, ruling over 6,660,000 demons; another, Johan Weyer, the sixteenth-century German physician, argued that there were, all told, 7,405,926 demons, governed by 72 princes of Hell. Weyer arrived at this figure using an ancient formula: he took the Great Pythagorean number, 1234321 (a mystical number thought to embody certain arcane principles of the universe), and multiplied it by 6.

His method seems as good as any.

What was uniformly uncontested was that the demons were a huge and powerful force, with armies and parliaments, aristocrats and commoners. When Hell's battalions marched in parade formation, they were said to shake the very earth — demons riding on griffins and camels, rattling their weapons and howling with rage, bent on destruction, revenge, and bloodshed. In one conversation, attested to by three monks, a demon general pointedly observed, "The strength of our army is such that if all the Alps, their rocks and glaciers were divided among us, none would have more than a pound's weight."

HOW OLD ARE DEMONS?

The life span of demons is another topic that has come up for much discussion over the centuries.

Hesiod, the ancient Greek poet, based his own calculation on the average life span of the phoenix, a mythical bird of great beauty reputed to build its own funeral pyre and then rise from the ashes reborn. The phoenix, Hesiod asserted, lived ten times as long as a man, and demons lived ten times as long as the phoenix. Thus, he arrived at 6,800 years for the average demonic life.

In later years, Plutarch, the celebrated Greek writer and biographer, issued something of a corrective: observing that demons are, like their mortal counterparts, vulnerable to illness and disease, he amended the figure to 9,720 years.

Others simply assumed that, like angels, the demons were immortal and would be around until the end of time.

So far, the answer has remained elusive.

THE HIERARCHY OF HELL

*H*ow were all these demons organized? Who lorded it over whom? Who gave the orders, and who obeyed them?

On this, too, there has been much discussion — and little unanimity — over the centuries. One thing alone was seldom debated: Satan, also known as the Emperor of the Grand Grimoire, the Prince of Light, and the Angel of Darkness, was the man in charge. He was God's great adversary, the Serpent, the Snake, the Spirit of Universal Hate. In him, evil was incarnate and unalloyed.

But under him there ranged a large and terrible crew of demons and creatures, bent on mayhem and wanton destruction. Keeping such a horde in line was too much of a task for even Satan to handle alone, so just as the Lord had his seraphim, his cherubim, his arch-

Satan presiding over a witches' sabbat.

angels, Satan, too, appointed his own unholy aristocracy to help him rule over his kingdom. These demons, in an inversion of the nine-fold order of the angels, were sometimes divided into nine infernal orders of their own. But first among them, it is generally agreed, was one of Satan's oldest friends from his days in Heaven, a powerful angel named . . .

Beelzebub. When Satan first rebelled, he recruited several very powerful seraphim, Beelzebub among them, to fight at his side. Once he took up his new residence in Hell, Beelzebub learned to tempt men with pride. When summoned by witches or sorcerers, he appeared in the form of a fly, because "Lord of the Flies" was his nom de guerre, as it were. He'd acquired it by visiting a plague of flies upon the harvest of Canaan, or, perhaps, simply because flies were once believed to be generated in the flesh of decaying corpses. Either way, the name stuck.

Another great angel that plummeted from Heaven in Lucifer's company was **Leviathan,** characterized in Isaiah 27:1 as "that crooked serpent . . . the dragon that is in the sea." By some accounts, Leviathan is credited — or blamed, to be more precise —with being the serpent who seduced Eve in the Garden of Eden. In Hell he might be considered Secretary of the Navy, as Satan put him in charge of all the maritime regions.

Asmodeus was one of the busiest demons. He was not only the overseer of all the gambling houses in the court of Hell, but the general spreader of dissipation. On top of that, Asmodeus was the demon of lust, personally responsible for stirring up matrimonial trouble. Maybe it was because he came from the original dysfunctional family. According to Jewish legend, his mother was a mortal woman, Naamah, and his father was one of the fallen angels. (Or, possibly, Adam before Eve came along.) Characterized in *The Testament of Solomon,* the great manual of magic, as "furious and shouting," Asmodeus routinely did everything he could to keep husbands and wives from having intercourse, while encouraging them at every turn to indulge their pent-up drives in adulterous and sinful affairs. When he condescended to appear before a mortal, he did so riding a dragon, armed with a spear; he had three heads — one a bull's, one a ram's, and one a man's — as all three of these were considered lecherous creatures by nature. His feet, on the same theory, were those of a cock.

Astaroth also rode around on a dragon, but he had only one head — usually depicted as quite ugly — and carried a viper in his left hand. Grand Duke of the western regions of Hell, he was also Treasurer of the whole place. The original couch potato, he encouraged men to sloth and idleness. In his spare time, he served as a kind of guidance counselor for other fallen angels.

Behemoth, as his name suggests, was a huge demon, usually depicted as an elephant with a big round belly, waddling on two feet. He presided over the gluttonous feasts in Hell. As this probably kept him up most of the night anyway, he was made the infernal watchman. He also enjoyed a certain renown for his singing.

Belial was one of Satan's most venerable demons. In fact, before the New Testament firmly established Satan as the leader of the forces of evil, Belial had filled the position. In one of the Dead Sea Scrolls, *The War of the Sons of Light and the Sons of Darkness,* Belial is the uncontested ruler of the dark side: "But for corruption thou hast made Belial, an angel of hostility. All his dominion is in darkness, and his purpose is to bring about wickedness and guilt." Eventually, he moved down in the world, though he still retained his unofficial title as the demon of lies. It was as such that Milton immortalized him in *Paradise Lost* (Book II):

> "A fairer person lost not Heaven; he seemed
> For dignity composed and high exploit:
> But all was false and hollow; though his tongue
> Dropped manna, and could make the worse appear
> The better reason, to perplex and dash
> Maturest counsels: for his thoughts were low;
> To vice industrious, but to noble deeds
> Timorous and slothful."

When the notorious mass murderer Gilles de Rais attempted to raise some demons (using the severed body parts of a child he had killed), it was Beelzebub and Belial he was after.

THE GEOGRAPHY OF HELL

*E*ven demons had to have a home, and Hell was the one that God had chosen for them, "fraught with fire unquenchable," as Milton put it, "the house of woe and pain."

Still, Satan and his crew did what they could with the place, exploring its vast wastelands, enduring its torments, even erecting some towering monuments of their own there. The infernal regions have always been a challenge — tough to live in, tougher still to get out of. And, since those who go to Hell seldom if ever return, it's been an especially difficult place to map out. To get some idea of how the place is laid out, we have had to rely upon the accounts of saints and seers, poets and prophets. And over the centuries, the picture and the terrain have often changed.

In the New Testament, Matthew gives a taste of the place, while describing how Jesus on Judgment Day will go about separating the good from the wicked:

> "And before him shall be gathered all nations; and he shall separate them one from another, as a shepherd divideth his sheep from the goats: and he shall set the sheep on his right hand, but the goats on the left. Then shall the King say unto them on his right hand, Come, ye blessed of my Father, inherit the kingdom prepared for you from the foundation of the world . . . Then shall he say also unto them on the left hand, Depart from me, ye cursed, into everlasting fire, prepared for the devil and his angels . . ."
>
> (Matthew 25:32–34, 41)

The fire stuck. Over the centuries, Hell has become an increasingly variegated landscape — with swamps and bogs, iceflows and forests, deserts and lakes — but in every conception, somewhere, a fire has been burning. In *The City of God*, written in the fifth century A.D., St. Augustine went on at great length about the quality of the flames in Hell:

"Hell, which is also called a lake of fire and brimstone, will be material fire, and will torment the bodies of the damned, whether men or devils — the solid bodies of the one, and the aerial bodies of the others. Or, if only men have bodies as well as souls, still the evil spirits, even without bodies, will be so connected to the fires as to receive pain without bestowing life. One fire certainly shall be the lot of both."

In the Middle Ages, the abode of the damned began to assume an even greater definition — in part through a popular tract known as *The Vision of Tundal,* composed by an Irish monk in 1149. In this account, Tundal, a handsome knight and a bit of a rogue, falls into a kind of stupor at the dinner table. His soul leaves his body and is immediately assailed by a horde of gibbering demons. Paralyzed with fright, he is saved only through the intervention of his guardian angel, who offers to give him a preview of what he can expect if he doesn't mend his ways.

The preview is harrowing.

First, Tundal is shown a great valley strewn with stinking coals where murderers cook on an iron grate; then, fiery mountains where demons with razor-sharp hooks torment heretics and heathens. Next he has to wend his way past Acheron, a monster with flaming eyes, who momentarily eats him. (The angel, apparently, thinks this might be an educational experience for him.) When he manages to emerge from the belly of the beast, he has to cross a bridge two miles long and the width of only one hand; in the waters below, a thousand hungry creatures swarm. On the other side (he does make it across) Tundal meets a huge bird with a beak of iron, who eats him again, and then defecates him into a frozen lake. After climbing out of the icy water, and up the Valley of Fires, he is captured by a gang of fiends, who hammer him on an anvil with a score of other sinners.

When the guardian angel again steps in, Tundal is escorted into the depths of Hell proper. At the bottom of an enormous black cistern, he sees the Devil himself . . .

> " . . . blacker than a crow and shaped like a man except that it had a beak and a spiky tail and thousands of hands, each of which had twenty fingers with fingernails longer than knights' lances, with feet and toenails much the same, and all of them squeezing unhappy souls. He lay bound with chains on an iron gridiron above a bed of fiery coals. Around him were a great throng of demons. And whenever he exhaled he ejected the squeezed unhappy souls upward into Hell's torments. And when he inhaled, he sucked them back in to chew them up again."

Tundal, unable to shake this terrible vision, stumbles on toward purgatory, and a brief glimpse of Heaven behind a high silver wall, before suddenly awakening in his earthly body again. The minute he does, he asks for Holy Communion, gives everything he has to the poor and unfortunate, and goes off to spread the word.

Who wouldn't?

The most complete, ingenious, and detailed description of Hell most certainly belongs to Dante Alighieri (1265–1321). At the beginning of *The Divine Comedy*, Dante finds himself lost in a dark wood, threatened by wild animals that block his path. The shade of the poet Virgil appears to him and says that the only way out is through Hell itself, and Dante — the Pilgrim — reluctantly agrees to make the journey.

Hell in this account is like a great inverted cone, a dagger that pierces to the center of the Earth. At the top of the cone it's widest, because this is where Lucifer and his angels hit the Earth, like a colossal meteorite, when they were thrown from Heaven. Over the gates to the underworld are inscribed the words, "Abandon hope, all ye who enter here." Dante shivers in his boots, and Virgil comfortingly takes his hand.

And down they go. The vestibule of Hell is a great dark plain, where the souls of those who never really lived even in life, who took no decisive course, who "lived without blame, and without praise," flee endlessly from hordes of angry hornets. Dante and Virgil pass on and stop at the bank of the river Acheron, which flows all around the perimeter of Hell. Charon, the infernal boatman, ferries them across.

When they step off the boat again, they are in the first ring of Hell, called Limbo. Things here aren't really too bad. There's a meadow, a stream, a seven-walled castle. This is the place where Virtuous but Unbaptized souls reside, among them the great pagans. Virgil himself hangs his hat here.

But things rapidly get worse. The second ring of Hell is reserved for the Lustful, who are blown about forever in pitch blackness by the fierce winds of unquenchable desire.

The third ring is set aside for the Gluttonous, who lie on the ground beneath a pelting storm of rain and hail; Cerberus, the three-headed dog, barks incessantly and rips them limb from limb. In the fourth, the Avaricious and the Prodigal are divided up into two camps, and spend eternity rolling heavy weights against each other. Dante and Virgil hurry on until they reach a rushing current of dark water; they follow its course downward and into a dismal swamp known as the Styx.

Dark and dank as it is, even Styx is home to some: here, in the fifth ring, live the Wrathful and the Gloomy, either tearing at each other in anger or gurgling in the black mud below. Watching their step, Dante and Virgil take the long way around the marsh, board another ferryboat across the moatlike Styx, and pass from what is essentially upper Hell into the lower regions. If they thought they'd seen trouble before . . .

Now they enter what Dante calls the City of Dis (Dis being Satan), the Washington, D.C., of Hell, the place where the fallen angels kick back and relax. Here, in the sixth ring, he finds a wide plain, dotted with burning tombs; inside the tombs, Heretics burn.

Another river — the Phlegethon — must now be crossed, but this one is broad and filled with boiling blood. In its turbulence Dante sees the souls of those who have committed Violence — assassins, tyrants, warmongers. The shore is not much better, where Dante and Virgil must enter the dismal Wood of the Suicides. Here, the souls of those who have killed themselves take root and grow, becoming stunted trees with gnarled branches and poisoned fruit. Beyond this is a scorching expanse of sand, where those who have committed violence against God and Nature are showered with eternal fire.

Still Dante hasn't reached bottom. The eighth ring, home to Fraudulence and Malice, is known as the Malebolge. Shaped like an enormous amphitheater, it descends for ten more levels, on each of which a different class of sinner is tortured. Horned demons whip the seducers and pimps, hypocrites struggle to walk in lead-lined cloaks, simonists are wedged into stone holes, the soles of their feet licked with fire. Barrators, those who bartered their public office for private gain, are ducked in boiling pitch by a particularly frolicsome band of demons, known as the Malebranche (or "Evil Claws").

And even farther down, at the base of the Malebolge, is a well, guarded by fifty-foot giants whom Dante calls the Titans of Tartarus. Virgil commands one of them, Antaeus, to help them on their way by picking them up and depositing them lower down; Antaeus obliges. Dante is now in the ninth and final circle of Hell, Cocytus — the frozen marsh where the Arch Traitor himself, the monstrously sized Satan, is forever immersed up to his breastbone. His giant wings, with which he attempts to free himself, flap uselessly, producing nothing more than cold winds to freeze the ice harder. "If he was once as beautiful as he is ugly now," Dante writes, "well may all affliction come from him." Satan has three faces, one black, one red, and one yellow, with mouths gushing bloody foam and six eyes weeping. And while he weeps, he relentlessly chews the bodies of three traitors — Judas, Brutus, and Cassius — whose terrible crimes were still less heinous than his own. Lucifer betrayed the greatest Lord of all, and so he suffers here, in cold and dark, at the farthest possible remove from the source of all light and warmth.

Dante and Virgil escape from Hell by climbing down Lucifer's shaggy side — he's too distraught to notice them — and then crawling through an opening in the rock, into the clean air and starlit night.

In John Milton's Hell, as portrayed in *Paradise Lost* (1667), the same four rivers flow — the Styx, the Acheron, the Phlegethon, the Cocytus —

but there is also a fifth, Lethe, the river of forgetfulness, which seems to encircle all of Satan's domain.

By Milton's reckoning, Satan and his cohorts are "hurl'd headlong flaming from th' Ethereal Sky," plummet through the mighty void of Chaos, and land with a mighty splash in a lake of fire. No longer are they bright angels, and no longer do they inhabit the happy fields of Heaven. Their new home?

> "A Dungeon horrible, on all sides round
> As one great Furnace flam'd, yet from those flames
> No light, but rather darkness visible
> Serv'd only to discover sights of woe,
> Regions of sorrow, doleful shades, where peace
> And rest can never dwell, hope never comes
> That comes to all . . . "

When some of the more enterprising demons decide to explore this vast underworld, hoping to find some part of it that isn't quite so awful, they come up empty-handed — it's all either freezing waste, swept by wind and hail, or parched and searing plain, "a Universe of death, which God by curse / Created evil . . ." It's enough to make any self-respecting demon give up altogether.

But not Satan.

With the same pride that brought about his ruin in the first place, Satan takes stock of his dreadful new surroundings and decides . . . to build! An imperial new palace, to suit his station as sovereign of his own domain! As luck would have it, Hell is rich in minerals, gold among them. (Milton advises us not to be surprised by that; Hell may be the soil that best deserves "the precious bane.") Mammon, the demon of avarice and riches, is of course the first to spot the gold, and to excavate it with his crew. And Mulciber, who once built towers and battlements in Heaven, is now available to raise the walls of a mighty and glittering new palace in Hell, "Pandaemonium, the high Capital / Of Satan and his Peers." In no time, the underworld has a showpiece of its own.

According to Milton, the palace had many gates and porches, and a meeting hall as large as an open field, fit for jousting. And the decor? Opulent might be the operative word. When the demons assemble for their first council there . . .

> "High on a Throne of Royal State, which far
> Outshon the wealth of Ormus and of Ind,
> Or where the Gorgeous East with richest hand
> Showrs on her Kings Barbaric Pearl and Gold,
> Satan exalted sat, by merit rais'd
> To that bad eminence . . ."

As it was later interpreted by the English painter John Martin, the meeting hall of Pandemonium (literally, "All Demons") was a great curving amphitheater, with rising tiers and a domed ceiling lighted by scores of burning chandeliers. Vaguely Byzantine in style, with massive walls and galleries, towers and bridges, the capital of Hell was a palace meant to rival, in stateliness and scope, that of Heaven itself.

THE ARMY OF THE NIGHT

*N*ot surprisingly, Satan put great stock in his private army. He liked armies, and he liked what they were good for — war. When it came to death and destruction, what could beat a good uprising, a bloody revolution, or an international conflict now and then? For demons, a battlefield was like an amusement park. And Satan's chain of command was even more complicated than the Pentagon's; the main players were as follows:

Punishment for the sin of gluttony.

Put Satanachia, the Commander-in-Chief, had a profound knowledge of all the planets and provided witches with their animal familiars. He also had a peculiar power over mothers.

Agaliarept, a grand general of Hell and commander of the second legion, held sway over Europe and Asia Minor, and also controlled the past and future. Possessed of the power to discover all secrets, he was especially good at stirring up enmity and distrust among men.

Africa was under the command of Beelzebub's own lieutenant general, **Fleurety.** An expert in the use of poisonous plants and hallucinatory herbs, Fleurety worked the night shift, whipping up lust and the occasional war among men. He was usually accompanied by a rowdy band of his familiars.

Amon, a marquis of Hell, handed the marching orders to 40 legions of the infernal army. A demon who vomited flame, he had the head of a wolf and the tail of a serpent. He also had the gift of prophecy, and could see the future.

Aguares, a grand duke of the eastern regions of Hell, had 30 legions under his command. A master linguist, he was also known to incite dancing among mortals.

Amduscias, another grand duke, commanded 29 legions, and was known, strangely enough, for making terribly disturbing music. He was usually depicted as human in form, except for his head, which was that of a unicorn.

Sargatanas, a brigadier major directly under Astaroth's command, was uniquely skilled — he could steal into a human being's mind and share in his innermost thoughts. If he felt like it, he could then wipe out those thoughts, along with all memory, and carry the person off to another part of the globe altogether.

The field marshal on Astaroth's staff was a demon named **Nebiros,** who personally oversaw North America and often employed animals to perform his nefarious acts.

Raum, a count and the commander of 30 legions, was an accomplished destroyer of cities. He also had the uncanny ability to determine, in the event of theft, who the culprit was.

Baal, grand duke, in charge of 66 legions, was one of the most unsightly of Satan's officers. His body was short and fat, like a squashed pillow, and his legs, which sprang up all around, were those of a spider. His three heads were those of a cat, a toad, and a man wearing a crown. His voice was just as awful —raucous and shrill—and he used it to instruct his followers in guile, ruthless cunning, and the ability to become invisible.

In command of 60 legions, which he directed from atop a winged horse, was **Abigor,** a cavalier skilled in the secrets of war and prophecy. Unlike most demons, Abigor was usually represented as handsome and rather dashing.

Azazel was the chief standard bearer of the infernal armies.

PUBLIC OFFICE

*O*n the political front, Hell had its own prime minister, too, by the name of **Lucifuge Rofocale.** Lucifuge could only assume a body at night and he hated the light. Among his many duties were the infliction of disease and deformity, the creation of earthquakes, and the destruction of sacred deities. His powers extended over all the treasures of the Earth.

The grand president of Hell, a robust, white-haired old man, was **Forcas.** He taught logic and rhetoric, and commanded 29 legions of the infernal forces.

Leonard, a first-order demon, was the inspector general of black magic and sorcery — something like a quality-control expert — and master of the sabbats; when he presided over a sabbat, he appeared as an enormous black goat with three horns and the head of a fox.

Abbadon (Apollyon is another common spelling) bore the nickname The Destroyer, from his days as one of the destroying angels of the Apocalypse. In the Book of Revelation, he is identified as the chief of the demon locusts, which are themselves described as having the bodies of winged warhorses, the faces of humans, and the poisonous, curved tails of scorpions. His other appellation was Sovereign of the Bottomless Pit.

Adramelech, grand chancellor, was also the supervisor of Satan's wardrobe. Though he was chiefly a mule, part of his torso was human, and he had a peacock's tail.

Baalberith was the chief secretary of Hell, head of its public archives, and the demon who tempted men to blasphemy and murder. When seated among the princes of Hell, he was usually seen as a pontiff. He was also quite a voluble sort: according to the *Admirable History* written by Father Sebastien Michaelis in 1612, Baalberith once possessed a nun in Aix-en-Provence. In the process of the exorcism, Baalberith volunteered not only his own name and the names of all the other demons possessing her, but the names of the saints who would be most effective in opposing them.

Alastor was the executor of the decrees handed down by Satan's court.

Melchom was the princes' treasurer.

Uphir was Hell's physician, responsible for the good health of all the demons living there.

Verdelet was something of a cross between a maitre d' and a transportation coordinator. He was master of ceremonies in Hell, and also shouldered the responsibility for making sure witches on Earth got to their sabbats safely and on time.

Nysrock, a second-order demon, was the chef to the princes in the houses of Hell.

Dagon was the princes' official baker. Before taking up his culinary duties, he had been an important god to the Philistines — so important, in fact, that after they captured the Ark from the Israelites, they stashed it in Dagon's temple.

Paymon was in charge of public ceremonies in Hell, and used his own will to overrule the will of humans. He was a man with a woman's face, and carried out his public duties on a camel.

Nybras, an inferior demon, was in charge of pleasures in Hell (a thankless task if ever there was one).

Xaphan, a second-order demon, kept the fires of Hell stoked and blazing. At the time of the angels' rebellion, it was Xaphan's suggestion to set Heaven on fire.

NATURE'S OWN

*A*nd then, of course, there were a host of other demons, high enough up to have names of their own and special duties, but not exactly top-drawer. Many of these demons controlled natural forces, and wielded them, of course, to man's destruction. (What else?) Some of the most notable demons of this class were:

Furfur, who could control the thunder, lightning, and strong winds. A count in Hell, he appeared as a winged stag, with human arms and a tail aflame. Unless he was contained in a magic triangle, everything he said was a lie.

Vine, who could tear down great walls and stir up storms at sea.

Procel, who could turn water freezing cold, or scalding hot.

Seera, who could make time crawl, or speed up.

Abduscius, who uprooted mighty trees and crushed men with them.

Haborym, a duke in Hell, who presided over fire and holocaust. Three-headed — cat, man, and snake — he sat astride a viper, brandishing a torch.

Halpas, a great earl, who appeared as a stork, cawing in a hoarse voice. He was known for two things — burning towns to the ground, or building them up and filling them with soldiers itching for a fight.

PRIVATE DEMONS

*O*ther demons were even more direct in their attack on humanity. Rather than raising storms at sea, or brewing volcanoes on land, they took a more personal approach. They attacked the *individual,* sowing doubt and fear, jealousy and hatred, in his mind, or inflicting pain on his body. Of this unpleasant fraternity, some charter members were as follows:

Andras and his henchman **Flauros,** who went straight for the kill. Andras, a grand marquis of Hell, had the body of a winged angel, but the head of an owl. He rode a black wolf, and wielded a sword.

Shax rendered his victims blind and deaf.

Valafar, a duke, gave the orders to robbers and brigands who attacked innocents. He was usually depicted as having the head of a thief (whatever that was) and the body of a lion.

Sabnack caused mortals' bodies to decay.

Three confederates held sway over the dead. **Murmur** took charge of the soul, while **Bifrons** and **Bune** moved the bodies from one grave to another.

Philotanus, a second-order demon and assistant to Belial, specialized in prodding mortals into acts of sodomy and pederasty.

Dantalian could work magic on men's thoughts, changing them from good to evil.

Zepar entered the minds of women, and drove them to madness.

Moloch, once a deity to whom children were sacrificed, became a prince of Hell, where he received with joy the tears of mothers. His face was generally smeared with blood.

Belphegor sowed discord among men and seduced them to evil through the apportionment of wealth. He was pictured in two quite different fashions — as a naked woman and as a monstrous, bearded demon with an open mouth, horns, and sharply pointed nails.

Olivier, a prince of the archangels, tempted men to be cruel and unfeeling, especially toward the poor.

Mammon was the demon of riches and covetousness. He came into his own in the Middle Ages, based largely on Matthew 6:24: "No man can serve two masters: for either he will hate the one, and love the other; or else he will hold to the one, and despise the other. Ye cannot serve God and mammon."

Oiellet, a prince of dominions, had perhaps the easiest job of all — he tempted men to break the vow of poverty.

THE SEVEN DEADLY SINS

In their unending attempts to codify the demonic order, and demonstrate how the most infamous demons related to the best-known sins, scholars and clerics often made up handy lists for quick reference. Each of the demons below, for instance, was thought to be especially adept at luring human beings into the particular "deadly sin" with which

The demons of the Seven Deadly Sins.

he was identified. (These seven "mortal" sins, if committed with full consent, endangered the life of the soul; many other sins, of lesser importance, were known as "venial.")

One such list, which proved to be an influential one, was drawn up by Peter Binsfeld, a German authority on witchcraft who authored the *Tractatus de Confessionibus Maleficorum et Sagarum (Treatise on Confessions by Evildoers and Witches)* in 1589. In his rundown, you will note, the Devil is bifurcated into Lucifer and Satan.

Lucifer — Pride
Mammon — Avarice
Asmodeus — Lechery
Satan — Anger
Beelzebub — Gluttony
Leviathan — Envy
Belphegor — Sloth

This is not to say that the demons were unable to branch out and follow the path of least resistance. If one sin wasn't working—if a mortal was proving especially virtuous—the demons were perfectly capable of encouraging some other sort of depravity or evil.

THE GREAT BEAST

*A*ccording to the Bible's book of Revelation, something far more powerful than even these demons was yet to come.

> "And I stood upon the sand of the sea, and saw a beast rise up out of the sea, having seven heads and ten horns, and upon his horns ten crowns, and upon his heads the name of blasphemy."
>
> (Revelation 13:1)

This unholy monster, this great beast with the body of a leopard, the claws of a bear, and the fangs of a lion, was the bringer of the Apocalypse. Armed with all the powers of Satan himself, the beast, it was written, would hold sway over the Earth for three and a half years. He would wage war against the saints — and win — and lay waste to everything around him. With the exception of the few whose names had been entered into the Book of Life by Christ Himself, all the world would come to worship the beast and proclaim, "Who is like unto the beast? who is able to make war with him?"

And before long the beast, which arose from the sea, would be joined by a comrade in arms, who came from the land. This evil ally would be a false prophet — the Antichrist — and he would perform miracles and great deeds that would deceive people into accepting and worshipping him as the Messiah. He would teach people to make idols of the beast from the sea, and he would slaughter anyone who refused to offer such idols the proper veneration. Just to keep track of the faithful, he would mark them all, on their hand or forehead, with the number of the beast —666.

But all of the Antichrist's miracles would be tricks. Instead of bringing peace and love to the Earth, he would bring famine and plague, war and destruction. The Jews even had a description of what he would look like: bald, with one eye that was markedly larger than the other, a left arm that was longer than his right, and he would be deaf in his right ear (the traditional side of the good). Supported by the evil kings of the Earth, and his old friend the great beast, the Antichrist would marshal his troops against the angels of Heaven at a place called Armageddon.

And there he would finally meet his match. The angelic host, led by the Word of God mounted on a white horse, would rain down plagues of fire and blood and hail. With swords flashing, the angels would decimate the armies of iniquity. The false prophet and the great beast would both be captured, bound, and "cast alive into a lake of fire burning with brimstone." As for their secret backer, "that old serpent, which is the Devil," he would be chained by a special emissary from Heaven, then tossed into the Bottomless Pit. There, safely sealed, the inmate Satan would languish for a term of one thousand years.

A convocation of demons in Hell.

CAUTION:
DEMONS
AT WORK

"*L*ike one that on a lonesome road
Doth walk in fear and dread,
And having once turned round walks on,
And turns no more his head;
Because he knows a frightful fiend
Doth close behind him tread."

Coleridge,
The Rime of the Ancient Mariner
(1798)

GIVING THE DEVIL HIS DUE

*A*lthough demons were often characterized as vile and animalistic creatures, it never paid to underestimate them — or their master. On this nearly all the theologians and demonologists concurred. If the devilish hordes were truly stupid and incompetent, they would never have made such successful inroads into human nature, nor would there be so much evil and corruption in the world. Johan Weyer, the German doctor, offered this warning, which almost amounts to a grudging admiration of Satan himself:

> "Satan possesses great courage, incredible cunning, super-human wisdom, the most acute penetration, consummate prudence, an incomparable skill in veiling the most pernicious artifices under a specious disguise, and a malicious and infinite hatred toward the human race, implacable and incurable." (1563)

In 1580 Jean Bodin, the French witch expert, reminded his own audience that even the rank-and-file members of Satan's legions possessed great powers with which to beguile and seduce humanity:

> "It is certain that the devils have a profound knowledge of all things. No theologian can interpret the Holy Scriptures better than they can; no lawyer has a more detailed knowledge of testaments, contracts and actions; no physician or philosopher can better understand the composition of the human body, and the virtues of the heavens, the stars, birds and fishes, trees and herbs, metals and stones."

The devils could argue, the devils could reason, the devils could negotiate with the best of them. According to Catholic teaching, the demons were "pure" impure spirits, highly intelligent and self-motivated. Their will was bent on evil, on corrupting and damning mankind, but the methods they used were singular and in many instances remarkably creative.

CLASS WILL TELL

$\mathcal{A}$ scholarly pursuit, and useful pastime, for many centuries has been the classification of the lower demons (also known as devils) into different groups; the criteria have ranged from where they lived (in what element, for instance, fire or air or water) to what kind of mayhem they liked to cause (war, pestilence, madness). But one of the most authoritative systems was devised by the demonologist Alphonsus de Spina, who lumped the infernal legions into ten main categories:

"(1) *Fates.* Some say they have seen Fates, but if so they are not women but demons.
(2) *Poltergeists* . . . who do little tricks at night, like breaking things, pulling off bedclothes, making footsteps overheard.
(3) *Incubi and Succubi.* Nuns are especially subject to these devils.
(4) *Marching hosts*, which appear like hordes of men making much tumult.
(5) *Familiar demons*, who eat and drink with men.
(6) *Nightmare demons*, who terrify men in their dreams.

---

(7) *Demons* formed from semen and its odor when men
and women copulate.
(8) *Deceptive demons*, who sometimes appear as men
and sometimes as women.
(9) *Clean demons* . . . who assail only holy men.
(10) *Demons* who trick old women into thinking they are
flying to a sabbat."

Strange as that taxonomy was, another, which proved quite popular, divided the devils into their habitats:

SIX KINDS OF DEVILS,
AS FIRST DETERMINED BY MICHAELIS PSELLUS
AND LATER RECOUNTED BY FRANCESCO-MARIA GUAZZO
IN HIS *COMPENDIUM MALEFICARUM* (1608)

"The first is the fiery, because these dwell in the upper air and will never descend to the lower regions until the Day of Judgment, and they have no dealings on earth with men.

"The second is the aerial, because these dwell in the air around us. They can descend to hell, and by forming bodies out of the air, can at times be visible to men. Very frequently, with God's permission, they agitate the air and raise storms and tempests, and all this they conspire to do for the destruction of mankind.

"The third is terrestrial, and these were certainly cast from Heaven to earth for their sins. Some of them live in woods and forests, and lay snares for hunters; some dwell in the fields and lead night travelers astray; some dwell in hidden places and caverns; while others delight to live in secret among men.

"The fourth is the aqueous, for these dwell under the water in rivers and lakes, and are full of anger, turbulent, unquiet, and deceitful. They raise storms at sea, sink ships in the ocean, and destroy life in the water. When such devils appear, they are more often women than men, for they live in moist places and lead an easier life. But those which live in drier and harder places are usually seen as males.

"The fifth is the subterranean, for these live in caves and caverns in the mountains. They are of a very mean disposition, and chiefly molest those who work in pits or mines for treasure, and they are always ready to do harm. They cause earthquakes and winds and fires, and shake the foundations of houses.

"The sixth is the heliophobic, because they especially hate and detest the light, and never appear during daytime, nor can they assume a bodily form until night. These devils are completely inscrutable and of a character beyond human comprehension, because they are all dark within, shaken with icy passions, malicious, restless, and perturbed; and when they meet men at night they oppress them violently and, with God's permission, often kill them by some breath or touch . . . This kind of devil has no dealing with witches; neither can they be kept at bay by charms, for they shun the light and the voices of men and every sort of noise."

THE INCUBUS

*A*ccording to the church fathers, the incubus was an angel who fell from grace because of his insatiable lust for women. As a demon, the incubus continued with his carnal desires, preying upon vulnerable women, raping them in their sleep or provoking in them sexual desires that only the incubus (sometimes known as the demon lover) could satisfy.

Since demons, according to the traditional wisdom, were only spirits and had no corporeal form, the incubus was presumed to come upon his physical form in one of two ways: he either reanimated a human corpse, or he used human flesh to create a body of his own, which he then endowed with artificial life. Especially mischievous and clever incubi were often able to make themselves appear in the persons of real people — a husband, neighbor, the handsome young stablehand. In one case, a medieval nun claimed to have been sexually assaulted by a local prelate, Bishop Sylvanus, but the bishop defended himself on the

Incubi preying on a sleeping girl.

grounds that an incubus had assumed his form. The convent took his word for it.

So how could a woman tell for sure if her lover was a demon or not? There were a few clues. If she freely admitted the incubus to her bed, it would have the power to put everyone else in the house into a deep sleep — even her husband, who might be lying right beside her. Other clues were even more obvious — the incubus often proved to be a nasty lover, with a sexual organ that was painfully large, freezing cold, made of iron, or even double-pronged.

Occasionally, these unholy unions were thought to create offspring. Any children who were born with a deformity were automatically suspect. Twins were looked at askance, too. The magician Merlin was believed to be the fruit of demonic intercourse. And medieval records are filled with graphic accounts of half-human, half-animal creatures that were reputedly sired by incubi.

But even with all the attention that was paid to them, there never seemed to be a foolproof way of warding off these demon lovers. Sometimes prayer worked, sometimes exorcism and benediction, but in many cases, even these proved futile. According to Ludovico Sinistrari, the seventeenth-century Franciscan friar who authored *Demoniality,* incubi "do not obey the exorcists, have no dread of exorcisms, show no reverence for holy things, at the approach of which they are not in the least overawed . . . Sometimes they even laugh at exorcisms, strike at the exorcists themselves, and rend the sacred vestments." If they were suffi-ciently irritated by these attacks, incubi could respond with random violence and mayhem. When Sinistrari himself tried to free a virtuous matron from one persistent incubus, the demon gathered hundreds of roofing stones and with them erected a wall around the woman's bed. When it was finished, the wall was so high, Sinistrari reports, "the couple were unable to leave their bed without using a ladder."

THE SUCCUBUS

The incubus wasn't the only demon wielding sex as a weapon. He had a female counterpart — the succubus. In the view of most medieval theologians, incubi outnumbered succubi by nine to one, but the ladies made up in menace for what they lacked in numbers. Alluring and per-suasive, they used their considerable charms to seduce men and lead them to eternal damnation.

Francis Barrett, who in 1801 wrote *The Magus, or Celestial Intelligencer*, believed that succubi were either synonymous with, or descendants of, the classical wood nymphs: "And seeing the fauni and nymphs of the wood were preferred before the other [spirits] in beauty, they afterwards gener-ated their offspring among themselves, and at length began wedlocks with men, feigning that, by these copulations, they should obtain an immortal soul for them and their offspring." In other words, the nymphs tried to become a bit more human by mating with mortals.

What happened instead was that humans imperiled or sacrificed their own immortal souls by indulging in these sacrilegious relations. Saints, in particular, were singled out by the succubi: St. Anthony of Egypt, the first Christian monk, was tormented at night by a succubus "throwing filthy thoughts in his way" and "imitating all the gestures of a woman"; his disciple, St. Hilary, reports having been "encircled by naked women." When St. Hippolytus, who died in A.D. 236, was approached by a nude woman, he threw his chasuble over her, and she instantly became a corpse. (That's what she'd been in the first place, before Satan got her walking again.) And in one sad instance, reported by the Bishop Ermolaus of Verona, a hermit was so consumed with lust for a beautiful succubus that he fornicated with her again and again, and died of exhaustion within a month.

LILITH

*T*he succubus has a long and ancient history beginning, perhaps, with the Assyrian demon known as *Lilitu.* Sexually insatiable, this demoness prowled at night, looking for men to seduce and corrupt. In Hebrew myth, she was transformed and became Lilith, the queen of the succubi. Lilith searched for men who were sleeping alone, then seduced them and sucked their blood. She was also a great danger to children. Any boy under the age of eight, or any girl less than twenty days old, was possible prey. To protect them, parents were advised to draw a charcoal circle on a wall of the room, and write inside it "Adam and Eve, barring Lilith." On the door they were supposed to write three names —"Sanvi, Sansanvi, Semangelaf."

What did these names mean? For Lilith, they were family history. According to one of the creation stories, Lilith was Adam's first wife, made by God out of mud and filth. But the young couple didn't get along at all. Indisputably the world's first feminist, Lilith considered herself Adam's equal, and objected to lying under Adam when making love. When he insisted, she flew away — and Adam went whining to God. God selected three angels — Sanvi, Sansanvi, and Semangelaf — and sent them to retrieve her. They picked up her trail by the Red Sea, where they found Lilith carrying on with a horde of lewd demons; by them, she had already produced hundreds of little demons, called *lilin*. The angels relayed God's order — that she return forthwith to Adam — but Lilith refused. In a gesture of compromise, however, she did swear that if she saw the angels' names written anywhere near a newborn, she'd spare that baby's life. The angels took the deal.

When Isaiah speaks of "the night hag," who dwells in the wilderness with wild beasts and hyenas, it is Lilith he is referring to. And it's Lilith in

Psalms 91:5, too, when we are promised God will protect us from "the terror by night."

LAMIA

*B*ut Lilith wasn't the only female demon prowling the night and preying on children. She had an equally ancient cohort in Lamia, a cave-dwelling vampire who made her first appearance in Greek mythology.

The original Lamia was the Queen of Libya, a beautiful woman by whom Zeus had fathered children. But when Hera, the wife of Zeus, found out about it, she forced the queen to devour them. Lamia did it — it wasn't easy to defy the empress of the gods — but ever after she haunted the night, robbing other mothers of their own children. These she would rake with her clawlike nails, before draining their bodies of blood. Once a lovely queen, Lamia had become a hideous beast, with the ability to change shape at will. She was known, too, for her extraordinary vigilance — when she slept, she took the eyes out of her head, so that they could remain on guard.

She also went, as it were, from one to many — over time her name came to refer to witches who were thought to steal children, and to female demons who could, while beautifully disguised, seduce unwitting men with their ardor. It was only after the men had been spent of passion that the Lamia also deprived them of their blood — and lives.

THE MARE

*I*n sleep, it is common enough to feel a shortness of breath, or congestion in the chest. But these feelings of suffocation were often attributed to a demon known as the mare; as these creatures customarily made their visits at night, they also came to be known, along with the dreams they inspired, as nightmares.

During the night, the mare supposedly perched on the chest of the victim, squeezing the breath out of him. In *The Philosophy of Sleep*, written in 1830 by Robert Macnish, the mare at work was described thus: "A monstrous hag squatting upon his breast — mute, motionless, and malignant; an incarnation of the evil spirit — whose intolerable weight crushes the breath out of his body and whose fixed, deadly, incessant stare petrifies him with horror and makes his very existence insufferable."

Fair young maids were also quite vulnerable to attack. As Erasmus Darwin (1731–1802) wrote:

> "So on his nightmare, through the evening fog,
>   Flits the squat fiend o'er fen, lake, and bog;
>   Seeks some love-wildered maid with sleep oppressed,
>   Alights, and grinning sits upon her breast . . .

Back o'er her pillow sinks her blushing head,
Her snow-white limbs hang helpless from the bed;
While with quick sighs and suffocative breath
Her interrupted heart pulse swims in death."

Finally, horses, too, were considered to be in danger from the mare. But for some reason a stone hung up in the stables would protect them.

THE DREAM LOVER

In 1698 Johann Klein, a professor of law at the University of Rostock in eastern Germany, recounted the story of Mme. de Montleon, a woman who claimed her husband came to her, and impregnated her, in a dream. It would have had to be in a dream: her husband, the nobleman Jerome Auguste de Montleon, had been away from home for four years, and he died before returning. But shortly after his death, a son was born, and Madame insisted that the boy was the rightful heir to his father's estate. A lower court begged to differ, but the case was appealed to the Parlement of Grenoble; there, midwives and doctors testified that such dream-impregnations were not only possible, but commonplace. Based on their testimony, the Parlement accepted Mme. de Montleon's account, though the faculty of the Sorbonne in Paris, taking their own look at the case, came to the conclusion that the Parlement was just being kind to a lady in a difficult spot.

IMPS

*W*hat guardian angels are to those who live righteously, imps are to those who follow Satan; they are the errand boys of evil. Small in size — Paracelsus, the medieval physician and alchemist, reputedly kept one sealed in the crystal pommel of his sword — they are employed to perform everything from pranks to murder.

Not surprisingly, witches had a particular fondness for imps, keeping them as their familiars. Indeed, when Mary Scrutten of Framlingham confessed to her witchcraft, she admitted that she kept three imps, and suckled them in her bed at night. She had tried to allay her husband's suspicions by telling him that they were mice, but he had remained unpersuaded.

Imps took all sorts of shapes — some looked like tiny humans, others looked like toads or moles. Low-maintenance demons, they could be kept anywhere — bottles were a popular place to store the smaller ones — but they did have to be fed. Mrs. Heard in 1582 said she provided hers with "wheat, barley, oats, bread and cheese . . . and water and beer to drink." Margaret Cotton in 1602 said her imps liked roasted apples and claret wine. And Anne Bodenham in 1651 said hers were kept content with only crumbs of bread.

But there was one dietary supplement that all imps required without fail — and that was blood.

Henry Hallywell, a Master of Arts at Cambridge University, offered a scientific explanation for this sanguinary addiction in his *Melampronoea,* published in 1681. The imps, he reasoned, "being so mightily debauched . . . wear away by a continual deflux of particles, and therefore require some nutriment to supply the place of the fugacious atoms, which is done by sucking the blood and spirits of these forlorn wretches (their witch mistresses) . . . And no doubt but that these impure devils may take as much pleasure in sucking the warm blood of men or beasts, as a cheerful and healthy constitution in drawing in the refreshing gales of pure and sincere air!"

That, at least, was the medical explanation.

For anyone still intent on conjuring up an imp of his own, another book, an eighteenth-century grimoire entitled *Secret des Secrets*, offered the following formula. The imp, it advised, "was called forth by God, by Jesus, by the Holy Trinity, by the virginity of the Holy Virgin, by the four holy words God spoke to Moses (Io, Zati, Zata, Abata) and by the nine heavens"; he was admonished to appear "visibly and without delay in a fair human form, not terrifying, without or within this phial, which holds water prepared to receive thee."

GHOULS

*O*ne of the most unsavory lot of evil creatures, surpassing even the demons with whom they were commonly associated, were the *ghouls.*

Derived from the Arabic word *ghul,* ghouls were thought to dwell in dark and lonely places, the shadows, the desert, the bleak and parched mountains, where they would leap out and seize their prey at night. In Middle Eastern stories, they fed on small children . . . and corpses. In the traditional Western literature, they gradually came to haunt graveyards in particular, unearthing the freshly interred bodies and feeding upon them.

But even a ghoul could assume, under certain circumstances, a pleasing disguise and demeanor. In one account, from the fifteenth century, there was an elderly merchant in Baghdad, who had only one son. To this son, named Abdul-Hassan, the merchant was leaving his entire fortune. But the boy was still unmarried, and to make sure he would be well cared for, the merchant decided to arrange for his marriage. As a bride, he chose the daughter of a fellow merchant, a man with whom he had often traveled. But when he told Abdul about the planned nuptials, and showed him a picture of his bride-to-be, the son — who had never before defied his father's wishes — asked for some time to consider. The girl wasn't at all pretty, and the boy didn't know what to do.

One night, while thinking about his dilemma, he went walking in the outskirts of the city. From a grove, he heard the sound of a woman singing — the most beautiful singing he had ever heard — and he quickly stole up to the trees. What he saw there was a humble house with a vine-laden balcony, and on the balcony he saw a beautiful young girl, quite unaware of his presence.

Abdul was instantly enraptured by her.

The next day he hurried right back to the place, asked some questions of people passing by, and learned that the girl was seventeen years old, unbetrothed, and very well brought up. Her name was Nadilla, and her father, though a wise man, was quite poor. That, he knew, wouldn't sit well with his father, but he was determined to try his luck anyway.

He went to his father and spilled his heart. He didn't want to marry the merchant's daughter, he said, he wanted to marry a girl he had discovered on his own, a girl he couldn't get out of his thoughts. His father, predictably, argued at first, but then, seeing how intent Abdul was, relented; he met with the wise man and asked that the daughter be married to his son. The wise man agreed, the young people were now properly introduced, and they promptly fell in love with each other.

For the next several months, the newlyweds were very happy with each other . . . until one night when Abdul awoke and found himself alone. He waited in the dark for his wife's return, growing more anxious all the time, but it wasn't until just before dawn that she slipped back into the room, with a strange look on her face. Abdul pretended to be asleep.

The next night, it happened again. But this time Abdul jumped into his clothes and followed her at a safe distance. To his horror, he saw her turn into the cemetery, then descend into a tomb lighted by three funerary lamps. He crept closer and looked inside . . . where he saw his lovely young wife laughing, singing, and feasting with several hideous ghouls. As he watched, speechless, a freshly buried corpse was brought in, cut into pieces, and shared out among the revelers. When they were done eating, they gathered up the picked-clean bones and once again interred them.

Abdul raced home, and feigned sleep when Nadilla returned. At dinner that evening he pressed food upon her but, as she always did at the dinner table, she declined. Abdul tried again, she refused, and in anger he cried out, "I suppose you prefer to eat with the ghouls!"

Nadilla didn't say a word. She stood up, left the room, and got into the bed. In the middle of the night, when she thought her husband was fast asleep, she leapt on his chest, tore at the veins in his neck, and tried to suck his blood. But Abdul threw her off, grabbed a dagger he'd kept close, and stabbed her. She died on the bedroom floor, and her body was buried the next day.

Three nights later she returned, and Abdul had to fight her off again.

Her tomb was reopened, and her body, to all appearances, was as fresh and uncorrupted as it had been in life. When Abdul demanded an explanation from her father, the old man confessed that she had been married once before, to one of the Caliph's officers, who had introduced her to terrible debaucheries and then murdered her. She had come back to life that time, too, and returned home.

When Abdul heard this, he knew there was nothing else he could do but destroy the body altogether. He built a pyre of scented wood, laid the beautiful Nadilla on top, and set it afire. And when the fire went out, he took the cinders and ash and cast them into the swirling waters of the Tigris.

THE GOLEM

In Jewish folklore, the golem is a creature fashioned from red clay, inspired with life through magic, and made to do his master's will. But as with many such creatures that appear also in Greek and Arab legend, the golem often had a problem doing as he was told.

Crafted in the shape of a man, the golem was invested with life when the name of God was pronounced over him, and the word *emeth* (truth) was written on his forehead. Once alive, the golem was mute but powerful, and served as a kind of willing automaton. His job was to do heavy labor and household chores, but he was never under any circumstances to leave the house. The problem with many golems was that they grew; they got bigger and stronger all the time, and soon it became difficult if not impossible to control them. To do so, one had to touch a golem's forehead — which became harder and harder to reach — and rub out the first letter of the word there. When *emeth* was thus reduced to *meth* (he is dead), the golem immediately lost his vital force, crumbling back into the clay he was made from.

The golem's most famous appearance was in sixteenth-century Prague, where legend has it that Rabbi Judah Loew ben Bezaleel created a golem to help guard the members of the Jewish community from plots against them, particularly the dangerous charges of ritual murder with which Jews were often maligned. Unlike most golems, this one was not only strong but clever, and according to the legend, did his job well.

But another part of the legend recounts how the rabbi's golem ultimately went berserk, and had in the end to be destroyed.

Because all creatures must rest on the Jewish Sabbath, the rabbi regularly reduced his golem to clay again each Friday. But one Friday dusk, he forgot to do so. The congregation was in the synagogue and had just finished reciting the Ninety-second Psalm when a great commotion was heard in the streets. The golem was running wild, rattling whole houses, destroying everything in his path. The rabbi ran outside into the evening streets, charged up to the rampaging golem, and wiped away the magic word from his forehead. The golem collapsed, and the rabbi ordered its dust to be gathered together and buried in the attic of the synagogue. Years later, one of the rabbi's eminent successors was said to have gone up to the attic to see what remained of the golem for himself. When he came down, somewhat shaken, he issued an order that no one else, in this or any future generation, must ever go up to that attic again. . . .

THE DYBBUK

The ancient Jews believed in another supernatural creature, too, though this one was incorporeal.

According to the Cabalistic-Chassidic conceptions of the universe and its mysteries, souls that were still burdened with sin were doomed to wander this earth for a time before finding rest. But while they were wandering, these souls were afflicted by evil spirits; to escape them, these unclean souls, known as dybbuks, sometimes took unwelcome refuge in the bodies of pious men and women whom the demons could not harm. Once they had possessed their victims, the dybbuks used their newfound bodies to complete the things they had failed to do in previous transmigrations.

As in the Christian tradition, ridding someone of a dybbuk required holy men to perform a ritual exorcism.

THE HOMUNCULUS

A homunculus might be described as a golem in miniature. A man-made creature, fashioned in the human form, the homunculus was well-known in Europe for many years (Arnold of Villanova, a thirteenth-century alchemist, was one of the first reputedly to have made one) and may have provided the inspiration in part for Mary Shelley's *Frankenstein* (1818).

But the acknowledged master of the homunculus was undoubtedly Paracelsus, the Swiss physician and alchemist. It was Paracelsus who provided the detailed recipe for the making of one.

It is not a recipe you can whip up anytime.

The first step was to take a retort, or flask, place inside it a goodly portion of human semen, and then seal the flask. Once closed, the flask was to be buried in horse dung for forty days, and "magnetized" (a process that is not entirely clear). During this gestation, the homunculus—a tiny and transparent protohuman—was assumed to take shape.

Next the flask had to be unsealed, in order to begin the feeding of the creature. This was done by adding a dose of human blood daily, and by keeping the contents at the constant temperature of a mare's womb. After another forty weeks, if everything had been done right, you had a fully developed, well-proportioned human child, no longer transparent, though still very small. In time, he would grow to normal size. "It may be raised and educated," Paracelsus counseled, "like any other child, until it grows older and is able to look after itself."

Some of the ancient philosophers, such as Zosimus of Greece, and magicians, such as Simon Magus, claimed to have been successful in the creation of a homunculus. But as a result, they were sometimes suspected of being homunculi themselves. Anyone who could pull off such a formidable task, the standard reasoning went, must be a supernatural creature himself.

THE MANDRAKE

Somewhat simpler to make than the homunculus, though not without its own problems, was the mannikin, or elf, created from the root of the mandrake plant. Properly cared for, this little gnome could give invaluable advice and great wealth; but if it was neglected or scorned, its owner could wind up dead.

The mandrake is a humble plant of the Solanaceae family, along with henbane, belladonna, and tobacco. But it has an extraordinary history. Because of its thick, white roots, which are forked and roughly resemble the human trunk and legs, the mandrake has been invested with a whole host of supernatural properties. For centuries, it was thought to cure everything from madness to insomnia; its "apples" (the orange fruit that it produces) were considered an aphrodisiac and its root was used as a powerful talisman — so powerful that just acquiring a mandrake root was a deed requiring courage and a knowledge of the magical arts.

As far back as in the writings of Pliny, in the first century A.D., the mandrake was approached with caution. Pliny advised anyone hoping to pull a mandrake root from the earth to stand with his back to the wind, mark three concentric circles around the plant with a sword, pour a libation, turn to the west, and then, with the sword, pry the plant loose. If these steps weren't observed, he warned, the plant would use its forked legs to run away.

Flavius Josephus, a Jewish authority on such matters (and a contemporary of Pliny's), added something far more frightening to the formula: Josephus wrote that the plant shrieked when its roots were torn from the ground, and that the sound of this terrible cry could kill a man. Fortunately, he had a solution. He advised his herbalists to loosen the dirt around the plant, tie a string around the top of the root, then tie the other end of the string to a dog. Once the man was far enough away, he was to blow a hunting horn to call the dog, who would presumably respond to the call, pull the plant free of the soil, and die on the spot. Later accounts asserted that the mandrake could only be harvested at midnight, at a crossroads, beneath the gibbet where a man had been hanged.

But why all this trouble to acquire a root? According to one common practice, the mandrake was used as something like a Voodoo doll; witches could dress it up and make it represent a person against whom they wished to direct their magic. Wherever they injured the mandrake, it was thought the person would be injured, too. In Germany, peasants added millet grains for eyes and took great care of their little mandrakes — bathing them, dressing them, tucking them in at night (sometimes in a coffin) — in order to consult them on important questions. In France, they were considered a kind of elf, called the *main-de-gloire* or *magloire*. Often they were stashed in secret cupboards, because possessing one could be dangerous on other counts, too: it could expose the owner to the charge of witchcraft. In 1630, three women in Hamburg were executed on this evidence, and in Orleans in 1603 the wife of a Moor was hanged for harboring a "mandrake-fiend," purportedly in the shape of a female monkey.

BLACK BOOKS

*M*agic — specifically, the conjuration of spirits to do one's bidding — was a very serious, extraordinarily complicated, and above all dangerous business. And no sorcerer would think to undertake it without a black book, or grimoire, at his side. In these grimoires (literally, grammars) were contained all the secrets of the black arts, the rules and rituals and prayers that the magician must faithfully perform; if he failed to follow the instructions properly, he could find himself suddenly at the mercy of whatever demon he had summoned from Hell.

And demons were not known for their understanding.

The oldest, and the most sought after, of all these grimoires was something known as *The Key of Solomon*. And no surprise — according to one legend, it had been written by the devils themselves. It was given to Solomon, King of Israel in the tenth century B.C., and kept hidden under his throne. A powerful magician, Solomon was considered a master of the occult world; it was even said he had harnessed demons to help in the building of the Temple in Jerusalem. The book came to be called a "key" after the lines of Matthew 16:19, in which Jesus says to Peter, "And I will give unto thee the keys of the kingdom of heaven: and whatsoever thou shalt bind on earth shall be bound in heaven; and

Belphegor, an ingenious demon who seduces humans with wealth.

whatsoever thou shalt loose on earth shall be loosed in heaven." The book was considered just such a key, an instrument for opening the doors to secret wisdom.

Although references to the book can be found as early as the first century A.D., the oldest edition which still exists today, housed in the British Museum, is a Greek translation from perhaps the twelfth century. Many other editions, usually in French or Latin, were published in the 1700s.

But what does the book contain? In language that is heavily influenced by astrological and cabalistic doctrine, the book sets out, in elaborate detail, all the steps that must be taken to summon spirits and force them to do as asked. It prescribes the fasting and purification rituals that the magician himself must first undergo before even attempting a conjuration. Then it goes on to explain how to choose the proper time and place; the robes, weapons, and pentacles which will be necessary; the incantations, the drawing of the magic circle (within which the magician will be safe), etc. Though the spirits may be summoned for any number of tasks, they were most commonly invoked to uncover and procure the secret treasures of the Earth.

To that end, another book, also attributed to Solomon or his devils, was judged by some to be even more useful. Called the *Lemegeton,* or *Lesser Key of Solomon*, it was neatly divided into four parts. In the first, "Goetia" (or magical arts), it describes how to conjure up seventy-two chief devils and their respective ministers. In the second, "Theurgia

Goetia," it deals with spirits and their main characteristics; in the third, the "Pauline Art," it enumerates the angels of the hours of the day and night, and the zodiacal signs; and in the fourth, the "Almadel," it describes the angels who preside over the altitudes — as the directions north, south, east, and west were called — of the world. Like the so-called *Greater Key,* this one was purportedly buried under Solomon's throne, and only discovered after his death when demons, perhaps knowing that much mischief would thus ensue, encouraged his courtiers to dig it up.

THE BRAZEN VESSEL

*F*or Solomon, controlling the hordes of unseen spirits was not an impossible task: he not only had the Key to help him, but a magic ring that enabled him to give orders to angels, demons, and all the natural forces.

But since he was aware that others might find this same task quite overwhelming, he used his magical powers to gather together seventy-two of the chief demons, which he then forced into a brass vessel. After sealing it tight, he hurled the vessel into a deep lake, where he hoped it would sink and be forgotten.

But luck wasn't with him. The Babylonians, legend has it, thought the vessel contained some valuable treasure, so they went on a fishing expedition, found it, and, of course, opened it. Just as in the story of Pandora's box, the seventy-two demons, and the legions of their followers, flew out of the vessel and returned to their former places and business — except for Belial, who by one account set up shop in a graven image and in return for sacrifices and honors gave the people of the country oracles.

Among these newly liberated demons were some of the most famous and powerful, Baal and Aguares, Barbatos and Amon, as well as many others of more limited renown. And each had his own peculiar talent or propensity. There was, for instance:

Marbas, who customarily appears as a roaring lion, but who, if the magician requests, will happily assume human form. He can offer the same shape-changing ability to men. In addition, he can answer questions about anything hidden or secret, and cause — or cure, if he chooses — disease.

Sytry, a great prince with the head of a leopard and the wings of a griffin. He stimulates passion between the sexes, in part by encouraging women to display themselves naked.

Gomory, also skilled at procuring the love of women — particularly young women. In fact, Gomory, a prominent duke, appears as a beautiful woman himself, riding a camel and wearing a ducal crown.

Lerajie, a powerful marquis, who appears as an archer in a green tunic, armed with bow and arrows. He stirs up battles among men and takes a special interest in arrow wounds — which he causes to putrefy.

Glasyalabolas, a winged dog, who is the god of homicides. When not inciting men to murder, he can also be persuaded to teach the arts, the sciences, and the knack of invisibility.

Caim, who looks at first like a blackbird, then transforms himself into a man wielding a sharp sword. When asked a question, he answers — though it is not entirely clear what this means — in burning ashes. Once of the Order of Angels, he likes to argue, and if he feels so disposed, he can impart the meaning in the songs of birds, the lowing of cattle, the barking of dogs, the babbling of a stream.

MEPHISTOPHELES

*W*hen summoned to Earth by the renowned Dr. Faustus, the demon Mephistopheles answered with a line from *The Key of Solomon*: "Why am I called? And what is your command?"

Faust wanted quite a bit. A sixteenth-century scholar and dabbler in black magic, Faust wanted power and knowledge beyond anything he could find in the many books he consulted (even those dealing with the black arts). A doctor of divinity and medicine, he wanted the secrets that Nature would not yield, and the answers that philosophy and faith had not been able to provide. To that end, he had studied the books of occult lore, in Arabic, Greek, and Chaldean (the same books many of the clergy at that time studied). And when he had mastered the skills they taught, he went to the woods one night.

There, between nine and ten o'clock, he stopped at a lonely spot where four roads met and drew three magical circles in the dirt — the innermost for himself, the outer for the demon who answered his summons. At first, his incantations appeared to have worked too well; he was assailed by a host of devils, who gibbered and railed at the perimeter of the magic circle, trying to terrify him into abandoning his experiment. But Faust persevered, and eventually, he was rewarded with a demon who agreed to do his bidding. That demon, whose name comes from the Greek for "he who does not like light," was the melancholy but clever Mephistopheles.

The pact they made was this: for a period of twenty-four years, Mephistopheles would serve Faust in all things, and supply him with whatever he desired. But when the term was over, Faust would give himself up, "body and soul," to the devil. The contract was signed in Faust's own blood.

And Mephistopheles delivered. The doctor, who had always been a poor man, suddenly had untold riches at his disposal. His shabby clothing was replaced by silk and velvet finery, his house was filled with rare and valuable things, his table was laid with sumptuous foods and wines. Seven beautiful succubi were offered to him for his carnal desires. And his thirst for knowledge was at long last sated — in the batting of an eye, the demon escorted him anywhere in the world he wished to go, even into Heaven and Hell, opening all doors, revealing all secrets. The stories of the things Faust saw, and did, were told and retold for centuries.

In one such story, he summoned the shade of Helen of Troy (an event immortalized by Christopher Marlowe in *The Tragical History of Dr. Faustus* with the lines, "Was this the face that launched a thousand ships, And burnt the topless towers of Ilium?"). In another, it was the ghost of Alexander the Great he brought back to Earth, at the request of an emperor. For princes and their courts, he was said to have conjured up lavish banquets on golden plates, and castles with towers and gates and lakes — all of which then vanished in a flash of fire. And once, when ambushed by a troop of horsemen, he summoned up a regiment of cavalry of his own that routed and disarmed them.

But time passed, relentlessly, and on the last night of his pact Faust invited many guests to his house for a great feast. It was then that he revealed the secret of his astonishing deeds. As midnight approached, he retired to his room, there to await the servant who was soon to be his master. Outside the house, a terrible storm arose, rain pelting down on the roof, wind howling around the windows. At the chiming of the clock, his guests heard a frightening commotion in his room, the sounds of a violent struggle. But none of them dared to enter.

The next morning the body of Faust, torn and bloodied, was found cast on the ground some distance from the house — and his soul, as the bargain had dictated, now belonged to Mephistopheles.

GILLES DE RAIS

In October 1440, a French ecclesiastical court was convened for the trial of one of the country's most powerful noblemen. The nobleman, it was charged, had "adored and sacrificed to spirits, conjured them and made others conjure them, and wished to make a pact with the said evil spirits, and by their means to have and receive, if he could, knowledge, power, and riches." Like Faust, this nobleman had conspired to use occult practices to fulfill his own unnatural desires. But he had also practiced abominations that have ever since made his name synonymous with human depravity and excess. His name was Gilles de Rais.

A handsome French lord who had once fought at the side of Joan of Arc, de Rais had inherited titles, lands, and fortunes that made him one of the richest noblemen in all of Europe. But he was a man of two natures — one bold and forthright, the other deceitful and corrupt — and in the end, it was his second nature that won out.

Raised in seclusion and luxury, de Rais had a brilliant career as a young soldier, fighting against the English; his bravery earned him the title of Marshal of France, and he was accorded the rare honor of wearing the royal fleur-de-lys. But at twenty-eight, he retired to his castles, his vast land holdings, and a new career . . . as alchemist, demon worshipper, and mass murderer.

Great as his fortune was, de Rais squandered it at an alarming rate, until he was gradually forced to begin selling off some of his properties, thereby diminishing his family's power and domain. To make up for the increasing shortfall, de Rais sought out the help of alchemists, with whom he believed he could find the way to convert base metals to gold. One of the men he recruited was a Florentine priest named

Francesco Prelati, with whose help he sought to discover the Philosopher's Stone (the secret material necessary for the transmutation of metals). But after many costly and failed experiments, Prelati told de Rais he knew another way to secure untold riches — and that was to conjure up the Devil himself.

De Rais was wary; he had no intention of sacrificing his immortal soul. But Prelati assured him that the Devil could be propitiated by other means. Prelati also claimed that he had gone into the woods one night and summoned up the Devil, who asked to be addressed thereafter by the name Baron. The Devil had promised him bars of gold if suitable respect and sacrifices were made. The sacrifices included the blood, bones, hands, and eyes of murdered children.

For de Rais, these were easy to come by.

For several years, scores of children had disappeared in the vicinity of his castles. Boy and girls, the prettier the better, were reportedly lured into his fortresses, never to be seen again. Despite the rumors, it was nearly impossible to press charges or prove anything against a peer of the realm. It was only after de Rais attacked a member of the clergy that the Bishop of Nantes finally took heed and moved against him. And it was then that the awful story came out.

De Rais had modeled himself on the rulers of ancient Rome, whose barbarous perversions he had read about in the illuminated manuscripts of his family's library. "I found a Latin book on the lives and customs of the Roman Caesars by a learned historian called Suetonius," he later confessed. "The said book was ornamented with pictures, very well painted, in which were seen the manners of these pagan emperors, and I read in this fine history how Tiberius, Caracalla and other Caesars sported with children and took singular pleasure in martyring them. Upon which I desired to imitate the said Caesars and the same evening I began to do so following the pictures in the book." By some accounts, de Rais tortured, mutilated, and then murdered over 100 children before he was stopped. He kept some of the prettiest heads as relics.

At his trial, dressed all in black, he admitted to his countless crimes, in full and lurid detail. At one point, his confession became so horrible that the presiding bishop went up to the crucifix that hung behind the judges and draped a veil over it; these abominations were too great to be spoken of before the holy icon. When he was done with the list of his atrocities, de Rais begged for forgiveness from God, the Church, and the parents of the children he had killed. The court, in return for his not recanting the confession, afforded him the privilege of being completely strangled before his body was burned on a pyre with two men convicted of acting as his conspirators.

Prelati's fate is unclear — by some accounts, he too was burned; by others, he was briefly imprisoned and then released on orders from the Duke of Anjou.

FAIRIES

A separate race of tiny creatures, seldom seen and best left alone, were the fairies. Also known to us as elves, pixies, or sprites, the fairies have, over time, come to be thought of as benign or playful little beings, hiding in flowers or granting lovers' wishes. But they weren't always so nice.

In the Middle Ages, some of the church authorities condemned the fairies as unmitigated devils. Others believed that they were the spirits of those who had died before their time, or the souls of those who were just a little too good to go to Hell and a bit too bad for Heaven. In Ireland, the fairy people were considered a part of Lucifer's host, fallen angels who weren't wholly responsible for their actions; true, they had followed the wrong banner, but chiefly because they'd been taken in by the Devil's blandishments. While the rebel angels were plummeting from Heaven, Christ raised His hand, and the most gullible (and therefore least culpable), of the fairies stopped short before landing in Hell. Some splashed down in the sea, becoming mermaids and water spirits, and others, who landed near towns and houses, turned into brownies and hobs. The really wicked ones — the Lucifugi — kept right on going, becoming gnomes and kobolds (in Germany) in the caverns of the Earth.

Though a few fairies were reputedly bigger than humans, most were thought to be on the smallish side — often just a few inches high. All of them were thought to have magical powers, for good or ill; so it was wise, whenever dealing with one, to proceed with caution and a fair amount of deference. Fairies were easily irritated.

In general, fairies were favorably disposed toward humans who displayed a cheerful, open demeanor. They put great stock in hospitality, and they were particularly fond of lovers. They hated stinginess. And while they thought nothing of stealing from humans — anything was fair game, from a pie cooling on a windowsill to a cow grazing in the field — they were outraged if a human made off with something of theirs. Once crossed, a fairy could become a dangerous adversary.

Some didn't even need a reason. They were just plain malicious by nature. In the Fen country, on the east coast of England, the Yarthkins were small and hideous, and always waiting for their next victim. The Border Redcaps of Scotland lived in tower houses, and wore caps dyed red with the blood of hapless travelers they had killed. The Highland glaistigs made themselves up to look like beautiful women, but sucked the blood of any mortal foolish enough to dance with them. The water kelpies sometimes took on the form of horses, but anyone who rode them was carried into the water and devoured there. Shellycoat, another water fairy, wore strands of seaweed and a necklace of clattering shells; like the will-o'-the-wisp, he drew the unwary into dangerous places, and sometimes, while "playing" with them, left them for dead.

The one common safeguard against the fairy race was iron — or, even better, steel. The denizens of the supernatural world have long had a certain antipathy to metal, in part because it has provided humans with such powerful weapons as guns and swords. Anyone entering a fairy's home was warned to wedge something of metal — a knife, a needle, a fishhook — in the doorway to keep the fairy from shutting the door. Hunters carrying home their game were advised to leave a knife stuck in the carcass, since that would keep the fairies from laying their own weight on it. Mothers who wanted to protect their babies at night hammered nails into the foot of the bed, or to be even more cautious laid the smoothing iron under the bed and a reaping hook in the bedroom window. Other ways of protecting the child were to hang an open scissors above it, lay its father's trousers across the cradle, or to draw around it a circle of fire. These maternal precautions were well warranted: fairies, according to the popular lore, often stole unchristened human babies and left one of their own kind — a changeling — in its place.

GOBLINS

*F*amous for both their mischief and their ugly faces, the goblins were fairies who seemed drawn to meddle in men's affairs. They were forever hanging around farms and villages, usually to no good purpose. Their skin was swarthy, or altogether black, and they delighted in scaring people out of their wits, stealing things from them, or even taking their horses out for a wild ride across the fields at night. (The next morning, the horse's mane would be plaited and tied into inexplicable knots.)

On occasion, goblins were known to perform routine household chores — though unbidden and unseen — and in return it was expected that the housekeeper would leave for them a bit of bread and a bowl of cream, close to the warmth of the hearth. There, the goblin could stretch out (though he wasn't very tall) and enjoy the creature comforts of which he was so fond. Goblins, and their French cousins the *lutins,* had a taste for fine wine and pretty girls.

Hobgoblins, on the other hand, were rougher, hairier, a little bit larger, and definitely given to country life. In his *Anatomy of Melancholy*, Robert Burton observes that they would "grinde corne for a messe of milke, cut wood, or doe any manner of drudgery work." In a good mood, the hobgoblin could act as a kind of guardian spirit of the house, keeping an eye on the servants, and watching over any hidden treasures: in a bad mood, he could drink up all the cream, stop the butter from coming in the churn, hide the necessary household implements. He could prove, as this seventeenth-century prayer by John Day attests, an unfriendly spirit:

> "Graunt that no Hogoblins fright me,
>   No hungrie devils rise up and bite me;
>   No Urchins, Elves, or drunkards Ghoasts
>   Shove me against walles or postes.
>   O graunt that I may no black thing touch,
>   Though many men love to meete such."

By and large, hobgoblins were thought to be something like the country folk they consorted with — slow and simple, with a penchant for practical jokes and broad physical humor. They were the hayseeds, so to speak, of the relatively sophisticated fairy world.

MERMAIDS AND MERMEN

The best protection against mermaids and mermen was to stay on dry land, where they were generally — though not always — powerless.

Human from the waist up and fish from the waist down, the mermaids, and their less common counterparts the mermen, lived in the oceans, lakes, and streams. The mermaid was usually described as lovely and alluring, with long hair and supple limbs; in her hands, she often held a mirror and a comb. And her singing was so seductive it could lure sailors to leap overboard. Once they did, the mermaid dragged them to her magnificent underwater kingdom, where their souls were kept prisoner forever. In Cornwall, the mermaid of Zennor charmed a lovelorn boy, the squire's son, into the sea, and for many years after that, the local people swore they could hear him singing, too, beneath the crashing waves.

But there were also accounts of beached mermaids becoming tamed and almost human. In 1403, a mermaid washed up in shallow water near Edam in Holland. The townsfolk rescued her and nursed her back to health. But she never learned to speak. For fifteen years she lived among them, and when she died, she was given the traditional Christian burial rites.

In Germany, bodies of fresh water were said to be haunted by nixies, green-haired maidens who could transform themselves into old crones and travel to town on market days. So disguised, they would lure their victims into dangerous waters and drown them there. To survive, each nixie had to have at least one victim a year. In the lakes of northern England, another green-haired maid, known as Jenny Green Teeth, had a special fondness for drowning children who trespassed in her waters.

To keep from succumbing to a mermaid's charms, it was a good idea to stop up your ears against her singing (as Ulysses did when sailing past the Sirens) or to somehow get hold of her cap or belt; if you had either one of these, you had power over the creature who normally wore them.

THE KNOCKERS

*B*etween the late seventeenth and the early nineteenth centuries, the crags and moors of Cornwall were dotted with black chimney stacks and engine houses, where shafts had been sunk deep into the land to mine the rich veins of tin, lead, and silver. The workers, who descended into the mines each day clutching a rope with a candle mounted in their hats, were well aware that they had company underground, company that they must be careful not to offend. These tiny creatures, who also lived and worked in the mines, were known as the knockers.

Often, the human workers could hear the sound of the knockers' tools, drilling and scraping at the ore, not far away — just around the bend, perhaps, or in the next tunnel over. Though it was considered unwise to disturb them, it *was* a good idea to listen to where they were working — the knockers, it was thought, had an uncanny ability to find the richest veins of ore. But if you spied on them, or attempted to make off with their ore, they could inflict a painful condition called "Barker's

Knee" — a sort of rheumatism that left its victims hobbled for the rest of their lives.

Still, one old man decided to take the chance. His name was Trenwith, and he was a miner in an area called the Bockles. On a midsummer night, he and his son lay in wait for the knockers, quietly marking off the hours, until they saw a crew of them struggling to pull their load of ore to the surface. With his hat in hand, and many apologies for disturbing them at their work, the old man approached the little miners and offered to make them a deal. Why should they work all night, he asked, when he and his son could do the work for them? In return for their showing him the best places to wield his pick, Trenwith would leave the knockers one-tenth of his haul each day. The knockers conferred among themselves and decided to accept the deal.

For a long time, both sides prospered: the knockers enjoyed their newfound leisure, and every day the old man left them their promised share. Soon, Trenwith was a very wealthy man. But one day he died, and his son was left alone to work the mine. Tired of honoring the bargain his father had struck, the son began to shortchange the knockers and keep the difference for himself. But the knockers weren't to be fooled. Angered at his bad faith and greed, they no longer held up their end of the bargain either. In no time, the lode had failed, and the son, who had squandered his father's money on drinking and carousing, was forced to go looking for work. Knowing that he had already defied the knockers, no one would take a chance on hiring him, and he died soon after, a penniless outcast.

GREMLINS

*A*lthough most of the denizens of the fairy world have been known to man for time immemorial, there is one — the gremlin —whose discovery was made only in this century. An airy spirit, he may have been hovering about forever, but it was only with the advent of airplanes that the gremlin truly came into his own.

"Ever since the days of Wilbur and Orville Wright," wrote one authority in a 1942 edition of *The Aeroplane,* "pilots have scratched their heads over the more obscure technical mysteries of aviation. An engine run up the previous night fails to start in the morning. The unaccountable leakage of petrol and air from tyres and brakes has always been a headache. . . . Only since the expansion of the R.A.F. has the source of the trouble been unearthed . . . Gremlin action."

It was over twenty years earlier that pilots of the Royal Air Force and the Royal Naval Air Service first noticed the effects of gremlin activity. Navigational controls would go awry, radios would go out, engines would stall, and a wing would suddenly and for no perceptible reason dip sharply — just as if a horde of malicious sprites had all at once weighed it down. As far as the pilots were concerned, that's exactly what it was.

Gremlins, they claimed, were living in underground warrens in and around the airfields. When no one was looking, they climbed aboard the aircraft, creating all kinds of mischief, and hitching a ride when the plane took off. Most of the time, they were just up to pranks, but on many occasions their fooling around put the crew and the plane into very real danger.

Just the sight of one was enough to make a pilot lose control.

About a foot high, and generally green in color, they had large, fuzzy ears and wide, webbed feet. The feet came in handy, first because they provided suction grips for walking on the wings, and second because they could expand, like parachutes, when the gremlins had to bail out of a crashing plane. Unaffected by extremes of temperature, the gremlins sometimes went naked. At other times, they displayed a marked taste for smart clothing —spats and top hats and red jackets embroidered with neat ruffles. Their favorite food was aircraft fuel, which they drank in prodigious amounts. (This explained how the tanks, which were thought to be full, could so often turn out to be empty.)

Still, the gremlins could occasionally pitch in when the going got especially rough. According to one Lancaster pilot in the Second World War, "One night we got bounced by a snapper [fighter] and the rear gunner was hit. I sent the wireless operator back to get him out of the turret

Lucifer

while we carried on the battle with the upper turret only, corkscrewing like hell." The navigator dragged the rear gunner forward, to get a look at his wounds. But while he did, the rear turret guns opened up again, blazing away at the German fighters and keeping them at bay. The guns didn't stop until the ammunition had run out.

After the plane had managed to land, the ground staff armourers carefully examined the rear turret, and in their judgment there was "nothing wrong with the guns or their controls and, in fact, there *was* no way in which the guns could fire like that." Shaking their heads, they chalked it up to a friendly gremlin — and the Group Armament Officer signed off on their report.

In recent years, it should be noted, gremlins have been branching out. Devoted to the latest technologies, they've started to invade all kinds of office and household gadgets, including televisions and, of course, computers.

VAMPIRES,
WEREWOLVES,
AND ZOMBIES

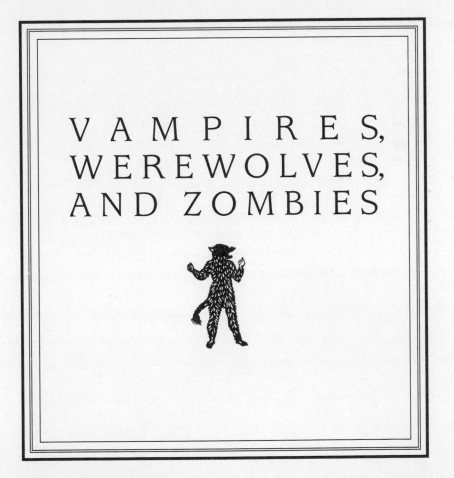

"But first, on earth as vampire sent,
Thy corpse shall from its tomb be rent:
Then ghastly haunt thy native place,
And suck the blood of all thy race;
There from thy daughter, sister, wife,
At midnight drain the stream of life. . . .
Wet with thine own best blood shall drip
Thy gnashing tooth and haggard lip;
Then stalking to thy sullen grave
Go — and with the ghouls and afreets rave,
Till these in horror shrink away
From specter more accursed than they!"

Lord Byron, *The Giaour* (1813)

A TASTE FOR BLOOD

*Gh*e vampire — a human being raised from his or her grave — and the werewolf — a man or woman transformed into a wolf — have much in common. To begin with, both are made of mortal stuff: they are not angels fallen from grace, nor are they demons (by all but one or two accounts) sent by Satan to tempt or corrupt mankind. They are, indeed, evil agents, but the evil they do is their own.

They share certain physical traits—hairy palms, for one, and eyebrows that almost meet — and both display a preternatural strength and agility. They share the ability to transform themselves (the vampire often assuming the shape of a wolf himself) and both use their well-developed incisors in constant quest of the same refreshment—ruby-red, warm, human blood.

The vampire needs this blood to survive, draining his victims lest he sacrifice his own eternal life. The werewolf relishes the hunt, as any wolf would, and he revels in the blood and flesh of his victims. The werewolf is a cannibal and a carnivore (making the vampire, by comparison, look positively dainty). But both, for their savagery, are cursed by God. And according to much of the occult lore, the werewolf, on his death, *becomes* a vampire. It might almost be considered a kind of bizarre graduation ceremony.

Partners in crime, allies of evil, the vampire and the werewolf have come down to us trailing a long history of death and destruction, their footprints etched each step of the way in the blood they have spilled for centuries.

ORIGINS OF THE VAMPIRE

*T*he word itself is of Magyar derivation, and much of the lore of the vampire, as we now know it, is of eastern European provenance. Bram Stoker, the Irishman who wrote *Dracula,* borrowed his story and background from the tales of Vlad IV, the original Count Drakul, a Transylvanian nobleman who lived in the fifteenth century and beat back the invading Turks. Vlad was also a sadist of epic proportions, who enjoyed the torture of his prisoners. Legend has it that Vlad often staged picnics amdist a forest of sharpened wooden stakes, driven through the bodies of Turks he had captured in battle; thus was born the nickname "the Impaler," with which he has passed into history.

He was no less a terror to his own countrymen. His castle, where people vanished, was loathed and feared. Within its high stone walls, terrible and sacrilegious deeds, it was said, were done, and at least one local account referred to the count as a *wampyr*.

His taste for blood apparently was shared by other members of the Carpathian nobility. In 1610, Countess Elizabeth Bathory was executed by order of the King of Hungary. A fancier of the occult, the countess had become convinced that she could prolong her own youth and beauty by bathing in the blood of young girls. Many unsuspecting victims were lured to her castle, drained, and buried. One of them managed to escape and tell the tale. The Blood Countess was walled up alive in her own bedchamber as punishment for her crimes.

From just such gruesome accounts, the vampire legend began and grew. And with Stoker's 1897 novel, it concretized around the image—part historical, part imaginary — of Count Dracula himself.

THE COUNT,
AS HE FIRST APPEARS TO JONATHAN HARKER,
IN BRAM STOKER'S *DRACULA*

"*W*ithin, stood a tall old man, clean shaven save for a long white moustache, and clad in black from head to foot, without a single speck of colour about him anywhere . . . He moved impulsively forward, and holding out his hand grasped mine with a strength that made me wince, an effect which was not lessened by the fact that it seemed as cold as ice — more like the hand of a dead than a living man. . . .

"His face was a strong — a very strong — aquiline, with high bridge of the thin nose and peculiarly arched nostrils; with lofty domed forehead, and hair growing scantily round the temples, but profusely elsewhere. His eyebrows were very massive, almost meeting over the nose . . . The mouth . . . was fixed and rather cruel-looking, with peculiarly sharp white teeth; these protruded over the lips, whose remarkable ruddiness showed astonishing vitality in a man of his years. For the rest, his ears were pale and at the tops extremely pointed; the chin was broad and strong, and the cheeks firm though thin. The general effect was one of extraordinary pallor. . . .

"I could not but notice that they [his hands] were rather coarse — broad, with squat fingers. Strange to say, there were hairs in the centre of the palm. The nails were long and fine, and cut to a sharp point. As the Count leaned over me and his hands touched me, I could not repress a shudder. . . . There was a strange stillness over everything; but as I listened I heard as if from down below in the valley the howling of many wolves. The Count's eyes gleamed, and he said:

"Listen to them — the children of the night! What music they make!"

THE MAKING OF A VAMPIRE

*M*ost vampires, according to legend or lore, are made so by other vampires: once bitten, they are themselves infected with the terrible contagion. They are at once invested with eternal life, and burdened with the blood-lust needed to sustain it. This begs the question . . . where does the chain of blood begin?

There are many theories. According to one, vampires are the reanimated corpses of anyone who died in a state of sin, unabsolved by the Church and consequently barred from salvation. In Slavic countries, anyone who led a life of wickedness and cruelty, or who practiced in secret the Black Arts, was a likely candidate; so were those who had committed suicide, perjury, or who had died under a curse by their own parents. Excommunicants were, of course, included. In other countries, such as Sicily and Greece, vampires were also recruited from the ranks of the unavenged dead: anyone who had been murdered could rise up as a vampire to seek redress himself.

Another old superstition, which made the rounds from Romania to China, was that anyone whose coffin before burial was jumped over by a cat (or dog, hen, or virtually any other animal) was turned into a vampire. As a result, coffins were carefully guarded while they were still above ground. And if the unthinkable should happen, and a bird should suddenly fly directly over it, the lid was pried open again and a sprig of hawthorn, or a clove of garlic, was placed inside; both plants were thought to have sacred or virtuous power. In the Balkans, a piece of iron was put into the corpse's hand. Evil things supposedly shunned cold iron just as they did silver.

In some regions, vampires were thought to be born that way. Any baby who came into the world with teeth was suspect; so was any child born with a pronounced birthmark, or harelip, which was likened to a vampire's snarl. But more than any one thing in particular, it was the appearance of deformity, or merely difference, that aroused suspicion — in Mediterranean countries anyone with red hair, blue eyes, or an unusually pale complexion was watched carefully for other vampiric signs.

VAMPIRE POWERS

*E*ven though the vampire was doomed to wander the Earth each night, satisfying a burning thirst, he was provided with a host of uncanny abilities to help him in the quest.

First among them was the ability to shed his corporeal form at will. The vampire buried in the earth didn't actually have to burrow up, like a mole, through six feet of dirt every time he left his grave; it was thought that he could simply filter up, through tiny holes, and coalesce, as it were, topside. He could become, if he chose, a wolf, bat, cat, rat, or even a fine mist. In one guise or another, he could scale any wall, climb through any window, or even seep through any keyhole. Unless the proper precautions were taken, no place was safe.

And no place was more dangerous than home. The vampire had a strong inclination to visit his own family members first — husbands their wives, wives their husbands. Young women went in search of their betrothed. And all vampires, male and female alike, shared a taste for young, healthy, and attractive prey. In theory, the blood of the young was richer and more restorative.

The vampire could also command many noxious and nocturnal creatures to do his will; Dracula kept a pack of wolves to protect his castle and warn off trespassers. And he could cast a kind of hypnotic spell that rendered his human victims not only unable to resist, but unable the next day to remember the attack at all. (This way the vampire could feed on one person at a time for several days or, if the person lived that long, weeks. The victim only knew he was suffering from bad dreams, and a kind of unshakable lassitude.)

And then there was the gift — or curse — of immortality. So long as the vampire was undisturbed, his grave undiscovered, and his blood supply renewable, he could go on feeding forever.

VAMPIRE PERILS

The sun was, by some accounts, the vampire's mortal enemy. To be caught in the sun's rays was to be incinerated. By other accounts, it was chiefly an inconvenience; the vampire was entitled to be out and about only during the nocturnal hours, and during the day he was duty bound to return to his own grave or crypt. This was perhaps the paramount restriction on vampire behavior, but there were many other rules to which the vampire also had to adhere.

The vampire could not abide the smell of garlic, nor could he tolerate a crucifix or other holy relic. He could not cast a reflection — and as a result steered clear of mirrors — nor could he, by some accounts, cross running water. Capturing him was next to impossible . . . but killing him was not.

First, of course, the vampire had to be tracked to the proper grave. Unless the telltale holes were found in the earth above a grave, all the bodies would have to be dug up in search of the one that showed itself still ruddy and complete. If the vampire had recently fed, according to some authorities, the body would be swollen up like a leech, or the coffin might be awash with blood.

Another method of finding the vampire's grave was to set loose a white stallion, one that had never stumbled or been to stud, in the grave-yard. The horse, it was said, would step over all but the vampire's grave.

Once he was found, there were several ways of dispatching the vampire for good. He could be shot with a consecrated silver bullet, or tied up in his coffin with special knots. But the tried and true method was to drive a wooden stake, with one blow, through his heart. This was usually followed by cutting off the head with a sexton's spade, then burning the separate parts, including the tainted stake, and distributing the ash to the wind.

Even then, vampires could prove frustratingly resilient. In the early 1700s, the Hungarian town of Liebava was positively plagued with vampire attacks. At the behest of the Bishop of Olmutz, an investigation was begun. As part of it, one man climbed to the top of the church tower and kept watch over the graveyard. One night he saw a vampire emerge from his tomb, dragging his shroud behind him. As soon as the vampire was out of sight, leaving his shroud draped across a headstone, the man retrieved it and carried it back to the top of the church tower. Hours later the vampire returned, and when he saw that the shroud was missing, he flew into a rage. The man in the tower called down to him, "I have it here! If you want it, you'll have to climb up."

The vampire ran to the ladder and scrambled up the rungs. But when he'd almost come to the top, the man pulled out a hammer and slammed it into the vampire's head. For a moment the vampire still clung to the ladder; then he lost his grip and plummeted to the ground. The man hurried down after him, and while the vampire lay insensible he cut off his head with an axe. The nocturnal attacks in Liebava ended.

In the eastern European market town of Kring, in 1672, the vampire was more difficult to dispatch. A man named George Grando died, and was buried by a monk of St. Paul. But when the monk went to Grando's house to console his widow, he saw the spectral figure of Grando himself sitting behind the door. The monk fled, along with everyone else in the house. But the figure was seen again, haunting the streets at night, tapping lightly on doors where it would not wait for an answer. It was soon noticed that at these same houses, death soon followed. And Grando's widow insisted that his spirit came back to her at night, throwing her into a deep sleep and sucking her blood.

The chief magistrate decided it was time to look into the matter. With a party of townsmen, he went to the graveyard, dug up the coffin, and opened it. Inside, they found Grando looking healthy and sound. He even had a slight smile on his lips. In shock, the townsmen all ran back to the town, and the magistrate had to round them up all over again. This time they brought a priest and a thick hawthorn stake, sharpened to a point.

The priest, taking charge, knelt down beside the corpse and held a crucifix above its eyes: "O vampire, look at this," he intoned, "here is Jesus Christ who loosed us from the pains of Hell and died for us upon the tree."

A tear coursed down the corpse's cheek, and as the priest continued, more tears appeared. The stake was brought forward, placed on the vampire's breast, and struck with a powerful blow of a mallet. But rather than piercing the body, the stake rebounded off it! It was struck again, and again it failed to impale the corpse. It was hit again, and again, and again, to no avail, until one of the townsmen grabbed a hatchet, leapt into the grave and hacked off the corpse's head. Suddenly the head screamed, the limbs of the body convulsed in pain, and the evil spirit vanished forever.

THE WEREWOLF

In past centuries, there was perhaps no more terrifying sound to the peasant in his cottage or the farmer on his lands than the howling of a wolf. The wolf was one of man's most dreaded enemies, a predator with great endurance, strength, and above all cunning. Seminocturnal, silent and sleek, prowling the woods and fields, the wolf was a relentless hunter with a prodigious appetite, and when a pack descended upon a village or farm, there was little that could be done to fend them off.

So it's hardly surprising that the werewolf ("were" was Old English for "man") should be one of the most frightening creatures in the great occult pantheon. Combining the savagery of the wolf with the intellect of a man made for an animal of fearful proportion, and the stories of werewolf transformations and attacks are ancient and many. One of the earliest comes from Petronius's *Satyricon,* when one of the guests at a lavish feast was asked to recount a recent adventure he'd had. The story he told was this:

Niceros, at the time a servant, was in love with a woman named Melissa, the recently widowed wife of an innkeeper. One night, with his own master away on business, Niceros decided to pay her a call and asked a friend of his, a soldier, if he'd like to come along. The soldier agreed, and the two of them set out in the moonlight. After walking several miles, they stopped at a cemetery to rest. Niceros sat on a wall, singing and idly counting up the headstones, but the soldier, without warning, stripped off all his clothes and laid them in a heap by the roadside.

Then, to Niceros's mounting astonishment, the soldier went on to urinate in a wide circle around the clothes, just as a wolf might mark his territory. And when he was done, he fell to his knees and was instantly transformed into a wolf. Howling, he ran off into the forest.

Needless to say, Niceros was terrified. When he went toward the circle, he saw that the man's clothes had turned to stone. Drawing his sword, he ran all the rest of the way to Melissa's house.

When he got there he was panting, exhausted, and white as a ghost. Melissa did her best to calm him down, then said, "If you'd come a bit earlier, at least you could've helped us. A wolf got into the grounds and went after the livestock — it was a madhouse out there." When

Niceros asked what happened next, Melissa told him that even though the wolf had gotten away, "one of the slaves put a spear right through his neck."

Niceros stayed the night, though his eyes never closed, and the first thing in the morning he set off for home again. On the way, he stopped at the spot where the soldier's clothes had lain, but all he found there was a bloodstain on the grass. And when he went, with his heart in his mouth, to visit the soldier himself, he found him lying in bed, with a doctor tending to a great bloody gash in his neck. "I realized he was a werewolf," Niceros said, "and afterwards I couldn't have taken a bite of bread in his company, not if you killed me for it."

FROM MAN TO ANIMAL

The means by which Niceros's friend transformed himself — urinating in a circle in the moonlight — was one of the oldest and simplest methods employed to become a werewolf. According to the folklore, there are many others.

There is, of course, the fail-safe method of petitioning the Devil. After sealing the pact — with the usual renunciation of Christianity, the rebaptism, the offering of a gift, etc. — the would-be werewolf receives

Behemoth, a demon of great strengths and appetites.

the power of changing shape, and sometimes a magic belt or some such item, which must be worn each time he does so. Witches, too, were sometimes said to metamorphose into werewolves at their sabbats. Whole assemblies of them were said to go on rampages across the countryside at night, and according to one old Latvian legend, the Devil himself — in the guise of a wolf — led thousands of them on a twelve-day march one Christmas.

Being born on Christmas day was not a good idea, either — it was considered an affront to Christ. In Italy, anyone born at the time of the new moon, or who slept outside on a Friday with a full moon in the sky, could become a werewolf. In many countries, it was thought dangerous to drink from a stream where wolves had drunk or to drink rainwater that had collected in a real wolf's footprint, or, God forbid, to eat a real wolf's brains. That was really asking for trouble.

But there were apparently people who did ask for it.

Anyone *wanting* to become a werewolf could perform the following ritual, in these easy steps: going to a deserted wood or hilltop on the night of a full moon, the supplicant draws a magic circle on the ground at midnight. (The outer circle is seven feet in diameter, the inner one is three feet.) Inside the circle, he builds a fire under a cauldron, into which he tosses a number of ingredients, including such old standbys as hemlock, opium, henbane, and parsley. He then recites a spell, a few of the lines of which are:

Wolves, vampires, satyrs, ghosts!
Elect of all the devilish hosts!
I pray you send hither,
Send hither, send hither,
The great grey shape that makes men shiver!

Then the supplicant strips naked and smears his body with a special ointment prepared for the occasion. Like the flying ointment witches sometimes used, this one was probably a mixture of things such as belladonna and aconite. (The blood of a dead cat was sometimes recommended, too.) After donning a belt made from the skin of a wolf, the supplicant kneels down by the fire and waits. If he's done his job right, an evil spirit will appear — anyone from the Devil to one of his minions — to grant the favor of werewolf status. (Why anyone would have made such a request, however, remains a mystery.)

To turn back into a man, the werewolf has, by most accounts, only to wait until dawn. If that doesn't do the trick, he can simply reverse parts of the ritual — taking off the wolfskin belt, for instance, or washing off the magic ointment in a running stream. Soon he's good, or bad, as new again.

WHAT DID WEREWOLVES DO ALL NIGHT?

*O*nce transformed, the werewolf could become either wholly a wolf, though an extra large and strong one, or a hybrid — a wolf with a man's hands, for instance. Either way, he spent the night hours in exclusively wolflike activities: hunting, howling, devouring his prey.

It was in his choice of prey that the werewolf differed from other members of the pack. The werewolf might pursue the same domestic animals, sheep and cattle and goats, that the other wolves did, but his heart wasn't really in it — the werewolf preferred human flesh, the younger the better. And given the choice, girls before boys.

In several famous werewolf cases, the perpetrators all confessed to the same cravings. Jean Grenier, in seventeenth-century France, proudly announced that he had hunted down and eaten many young girls (and was imprisoned in a monastery for his crimes). Pierre Bourgot, in 1502, claimed that he had broken the neck of a nine-year-old girl and devoured her. (He was executed.) And Peter Stubb, in sixteenth-century Germany, declared that he had made a pact with the Devil. In return for his allegiance, the Devil gave Stubb a wolfskin belt (or "girdle") which he had only to put on in order to change himself; an English pamphlet, printed in 1590, described him then as "a greedy devouring wolf, strong and mighty, with eyes great and large, which in the night sparkled like unto brands of fire, a mouth great and wide, with most sharp and cruel teeth, a huge body, and mighty paws." Thus transformed, Stubb roamed and ravaged the countryside around Cologne.

"He would walk up and down," according to the English account, "and if he could spy either maid, wife, or child that his eyes liked and his heart lusted after [werewolves were also known as rapists], he would wait their issuing out of the city or town, and if he could by any means get them alone, he would in the fields ravish them, and after in his wolfish likeness cruelly murder them."

When Stubb was finally captured by a band of men and a pack of baying hounds, he was asked to produce this magic girdle he claimed the Devil had given him. But Stubb explained that he had shed it during the chase; when a concerted search failed to turn it up, the townsmen assumed it must have been reacquired by the Devil. Stubb, who confessed to twenty-five years' worth of barbarous crimes, was tortured (the skin from his body ripped away with red-hot pincers), beheaded, and then burned. His head was mounted on a pole and displayed outside the town of Bedburg.

PROTECTION AGAINST WEREWOLVES

*I*dentifying a potential werewolf while he was still in his exclusively human form was considered the first and most obvious line of defense. To that end, people were scrutinized for such unusual characteristics as eyebrows that meet, long and reddish-colored fingernails, small ears that sit low on the head, and, not surprisingly, lots of body hair — particularly on the hands and feet.

Still, it wasn't possible to convict people on just such evidence alone; they had to be caught in their werewolf form. Then they could be cured, or, if necessary, killed outright. To cure them, the French (to whom the werewolf was known as the *loup-garou*) believed the werewolf had to be pricked to the bleeding point during the night. If, on the other hand, he had been made a werewolf by a priest's curse, he had to be cured through a wound, inflicted by that priest or any other. In some countries the werewolf could be saved if, in his werewolf state, three drops of blood were drawn from him, or his human name was called out. Werewolves who wanted to rid themselves of the curse had to go "cold turkey," as it were, and use their willpower to abstain from eating human flesh for a period of nine years.

Killing them wasn't nearly as hard as killing, for instance, a vampire. Once caught, they could be simply bludgeoned or stabbed to death. Shooting was also recommended, though by some accounts a silver bullet was needed. Wounded or dead, werewolves reassumed their human form (as occurred in the story from the *Satyricon*). A similar story was told in 16th century France, where a hunter told of being attacked by a huge and fierce wolf in the woods. The hunter fought the creature off, and in the struggle managed to sever one of its paws. The wolf fled, howling in pain, and the hunter, putting the paw in his pouch, started for home. On the way, he encountered a friend to whom he related the story. But when he reached into his pouch to show the paw, he found instead a woman's hand with a gold ring adorning one finger. The ring, to his horror, looked very familiar. He raced the rest of the way home, and as soon as he got there discovered his treacherous wife bandaging the stump of her arm. He turned her in to the local authorities, who promptly tried her, and just as promptly burned her at the stake.

CLOSE COUSINS: THE LUPINS

Though they were sometimes thought to share the savagery of the werewolf, the *lupins,* as they were known in parts of France, were generally considered a kind of lesser relative. Wolflike in appearance, these creatures haunted graveyards at night, howling at the moon and chattering with each other in a language indecipherable to man. When they got hungry, they dug up a grave and consumed the corpse. But if they were disturbed—if, for instance, a cemetery watchman approached—they would run away into the night.

It may well have been lupins that a French farmer reportedly stumbled upon in the early years of this century. Seeing the creatures coming, he scrambled up a tree and hid there. The animals lingered nearby, and he was able to hear them talking in human voices, though he could not distinguish a word they were saying. At one point in the conversation, one of them lifted his tail and produced a snuffbox, which he offered to the other. When they left, and the farmer climbed down from the tree, he found the snuffbox lying on the ground, and he knew the local man to whom it belonged. But he kept his own counsel for many years — telling the story, but leaving out who the werewolf was — until the man died. Then he told who it was, and to prove his case showed that the man's headstone bore fresh claw marks, as if made by a wolf, each morning.

Another legend, well known in Brittany, was of *Le Meneur des Loups*, the leader of the wolves, a sorcerer who gave the pack its marching orders. The wolves would assemble around a crackling bonfire deep in the woods, and listen to his instructions, given in a human voice. (The sorcerer could remain in human form, or take the shape of a wolf.) He knew which fences were down, what flocks were unattended, which travelers were taking what lonely roads after dark. Armed with this information, and often led by the wizard himself, the wolves were then set loose to wreak their havoc on the countryside.

THE ZOMBIE

*I*n other lands there were other creatures, other revenants, who rose from the grave. In the West Indies, African slaves created a strange, hybridized faith from mixing their tribal religions with elements of Catholicism. This new faith, which came to be known as Voodoo, featured an animated corpse called the zombie. Much of the Voodoo ritual had to do with ways of protecting yourself from zombies, and even more importantly, ways to keep from becoming one yourself—for that was a fate, truly, worse than death.

The funeral rites in Haiti and other countries where Voodoo is practiced (Brazil being one) are very elaborate; they are designed to ensure that the soul (or individual *loa*) of the deceased does not fall into the wrong hands. As soon as a person dies, his family calls in the *houngan* (or Voodoo priest), who comes equipped with a live chicken, from which he plucks a handful of feathers. These he places in a small white pot along with hair from the head of the body and nail parings from its left hand and foot. Together, these elements comprise the symbolic matter of the soul, and the vessel, called the *pot de tete*, is carefully guarded by the family until the day it is consumed in a sacred fire.

Then the houngan performs an even more appalling task; after asking the family members to stand clear of the body, he lifts the sheet and crawls under. He shakes his rattles and mutters incantations, and embraces the body itself, all in an effort to free the loa and capture it in a tiny bottle. According to Voodoo lore, it is often possible to see the body lift its head and shoulders as it allows the spirit to escape from its mouth. Once bottled, the spirit is entrusted only to a close relative, or possibly the houngan himself. By no means must it be acquired by a *bokor* (a kind of sorcerer), who will use it to create a zombie for himself.

Just how does the bokor do this? There are a couple of ways to go, though the exact ins and outs remain a bit mysterious. If he can manage it, the bokor can place a pot containing 21 seeds of *pois congo* and a piece of string with 21 knots in it under the dying man's pillow. When the man dies, the string turns into a spider and the spider becomes the essence of the man's soul. If the bokor comes to the door, knocks three times and turns his back, the man — now a zombie — will emerge. But the bokor must remember to threaten the zombie with a whip if he hopes to ensure its cooperation.

Another method of creating a zombie is simply to poison a living man with the deadly machineel fruit, or with datura, the thorn apple, and then once he's buried, to call him forth from the grave. Voodoo legend has it that the corpse must be spoken to by name, and must answer the call; as a result, many corpses in Haiti are buried face down, their mouths filled with dirt, and their lips sewn together. They're sometimes given knives too, with which to attack the bokor if summoned from their resting place.

It's unlikely, however, that a zombie would have the strength or will to defend himself. He is characterized as a mindless automaton, a human robot, that the bokor can command to do his will. In Haiti, zombies are reportedly seen slaving away in the canefields all day, without speaking or looking up, dressed in rags. They are fed next to nothing, watery soup or crumbs from the table, and lashed into continual, blind submission.

Even so, they are greatly feared. If a zombie is awakened from his spell, whether by eating meat or salt, or from hearing a living human call his name, his wrath is extraordinary. He runs wild like a rabid animal before searching out his grave again and trying to claw his way back into the dirt. The kindest, wisest thing anyone can do for a zombie at that point is to shoot him through the head (which effectively renders him useless) and then bury him again — this time for good.

THE CASE OF CLAIRVIUS NARCISSE

𝒥n 1980, a man entered the Haitian marketplace of l'Estere, approached a woman named Angelina Narcisse, and introduced himself as her brother, Clairvius. To say she was astonished is the least of it — she hadn't laid eyes on him for eighteen years—but the last time she had seen him, he had been in his coffin. He had been declared dead by the doctors at the Albert Schweitzer Hospital, and buried under a concrete headstone in the small cemetery just north of his native village.

And now he was back . . . with an amazing story to tell.

According to Narcisse, before he died his soul had been secretly sold to a bokor, by a brother with whom he was involved in a bitter land dispute. He remembered everything that happened thereafter. He remembered stumbling up to the doors of the hospital in the spring of 1962, feeling feverish and unwell, spitting blood. He remembered the next several days in the clinic and he remembered, with particular horror, listening to the two attending physicians declare him dead. His older sister, Marie Claire, was called, witnessed the body, and affixed her thumbprint to the death certificate. Still aware, but feeling as if his soul were somehow floating above it all, observing everything that happened to him but powerless to intervene, Narcisse watched as his body was placed in cold storage for almost an entire day, then removed and buried.

He remembered a nail being driven too hard through the lid of his coffin, and gouging his cheek. And he bore the scar to prove it.

It was several days later, still lying in his grave, that he heard the sound of pounding drums and chanting, and heard his own name called out three times by the bokor. Rising from his coffin, he was immediately beaten with a sisal whip before being bound with ropes and wrapped in black cloths. Unable to speak, unable to resist, he was forced to march, with other zombies, to the north of the country. By day their master made them hide in the brush; by night they marched on until they reached a remote sugar plantation where they were put to grueling forced labor. For two years, Narcisse recalled, he slaved in the fields from dawn till dusk, until one day a zombie who had been refusing to eat was given a terrible beating. Although such beatings were common, and zombies almost never offered any resistance, this time the zombie did. Enraged, he grabbed a hoe and killed their master with it. Freed from whatever hold he had over them, the zombies shook off their stupor and went their separate ways.

Narcisse, however, was unsure where to go — if he went back home to his village, he was afraid his brother might try to kill him again. So for sixteen years he roamed the countryside. One day he happened to hear of his brother's death, and it was only then that he dared to return.

There was no denying that it was indeed Clairvius — he passed every test, and was recognized by many of his family members. And even the death certificate, with his sister's thumbprint, was authenticated by Scotland Yard. But no one was all that pleased to see him: a selfish and contentious man in his previous life, he was even less popular now that he was thought to be — or, more properly, to have been — a zombie. Unwelcome in his old home, he lingered at a local medical clinic, or at the Baptists' cinderblock mission. And when, on occasion, he visited the grave he had once tenanted, where the cement marker still read "Ici Repose Clairvius Narcisse," the cemetery workers gave him a wide berth.

A riot of demons.

WITCHES
AND
WITCHCRAFT

"There, in a gloomy hollow glen, she found
A little cottage built of sticks and weeds,
In homely wise, and walled with sods around,
In which a witch did dwell in loathly weeds
And willfull want, all careless of her needs;
So choosing solitary to abide,
Far from all neighbors, that her devilish deeds
And hellish arts from people she might hide,
And hurt, far off, unknown, whomever she envied."

Edmund Spenser, *The Faerie Queene*
(1590)

THE WITCH

In truth, witches have been with us for as long as men and women have believed in magic. For as long as people have believed that nature and its forces could cure and curse, heal and hurt, cultivate and destroy, there have been witches. And those who called themselves witches have believed not only in the occult or hidden powers of the things all around us—they have believed, too, in their own ability to harness those powers.

In antiquity, witches had their own deities. In ancient Greece, they were followers of Diana, goddess of the hunt, and Hecate, goddess of the night. Medea, who made wax effigies of her enemies, was called a witch; so was Circe, who turned men into swine in her enchanted court. Witches could do good or ill. They were worshippers of the seasons and the skies, growers of herbs and plants, seers and astrologers and, in their own way, physicians. And they could be as easily venerated as feared.

But with the advent of Christianity, much changed. The rites and rituals of witchcraft were considered heathen practices, and by the Middle Ages witchcraft and all it stood for had become anathema to

Saul and the Witch of Endor.

the Church. According to the accepted doctrine, practitioners of witchcraft were ruled by Satan. The witch who had once performed ancient fertility rites, brewed herbal medicines, and predicted the future had degenerated into a creature of exclusively malign influence, a sinister agent of evil doing the Devil's work here on Earth. Her appearance and peculiar talents were neatly summed up, in one astonishing sentence, by an English lawyer, William West, in the sixteenth century:

> "A witch or hag is she which being deluded by a league made with the devil through his persuasion, inspiration or juggling, thinketh she can design what manner of evil things soever, either by thought or imprecation, as to shake the air with lightnings and thunder, to cause hail and tempests, to remove green corn or trees to another place, to be carried of her familiar (which hath taken upon him the deceitful shape of a goat, swine, or calf, etc.) into some mountain far distant, in a wonderful short space of time, and sometimes to fly upon a staff or fork, or some other instrument, and to spend all the night after with her sweetheart, in playing, sporting, banqueting, dancing, dalliance, and divers other devilish lusts and lewd disports, and to show a thousand such monstrous mockeries."

The witch had become — and has remained ever since — a frightful figure of depravity and sacrilege.

THE SABBAT

*A*lthough witches were generally portrayed as solitary crones working their magic in secluded cottages, they were also thought to be quite sociable — among their own kind.

Their gatherings were called sabbats, and by all reports these assemblies were something of a cross between a trade convention and a raucous carnival. They were occasions to meet, swap professional secrets, and indulge their most carnal appetites. (Men, incidentally, could be witches, too, though they never made as much of an impression. They are sometimes referred to in later works as warlocks.)

First, the witches agreed upon a time for the sabbat — always late at night, though at no particular hour. The place was usually a field or forest, a crossroads or a hidden cave. All that was really required was an open space, far from prying eyes.

No matter how remote the spot, and mountaintops were often chosen, getting there was not a problem. As part of their deal with the Devil, witches were given the gift of transvection — the ability to fly through the night air, on broomsticks coated with a secret flying ointment, on the backs of their familiars, or invisibly through the agency of the Devil himself. Even a piece of straw clutched between a witch's legs could serve to keep her airborne. They flew up their chimneys, and at miraculous speed straight to the sabbat. The only real danger was from church bells; the sound of their ringing could blast a flying witch right out of the air.

Once a witch had landed, she joined the other witches, who might number anywhere from several to a thousand. (The rule of the coven, a group of thirteen witches, was never strictly observed, at this or even more casual meetings.) But the first order of business was always to pay homage to the Devil, who generally attended the sabbat in his classic manifestation as a monstrous goat. Between his horns he often sported a lighted candle, from which the witches were to light their own. The witches were to approach him humbly, and offer what was known as the *osculum infame*: as Agnes Sampson put it at her trial for witchcraft, "the devil caused all the company to come and kiss his arse, which they said was cold like ice."

The Devil then took roll call, and recorded it in his Red Book. And each witch present was required to describe the magical acts and wicked deeds that she had performed since the last sabbat. When the Devil inquired what the witches were planning next, they told him, and he offered professional tips and guidance. Then he was introduced to the new recruits, who renounced Christianity and swore their eternal fealty.

If there were unsanctified marriages or unholy baptisms to be conducted, this was the time.

Then the merriment, such as it was, began. The banquet tables were laid out, and everyone sat down to eat — the Devil, with his favorite witch, of course occupied the head of the table. The menu could vary greatly. Some witches, such as those in Lancashire, said they dined on beef and bacon and roast mutton; those in Aix-en-Provence remembered bread, malmsey wine, and the cooked flesh of freshly butchered children. But one thing that was never found on the table was salt; because it was a preservative, it was thought inappropriate to serve it to agents of corruption.

Afterwards, there was dancing — back to back, which was considered indecent at the time, and moving always to the left, contrary to the course of the sun. The dancing, led by the Devil himself, grew more and more frenzied, until in a state of wild abandon everyone present threw themselves into a frantic orgy of perversion. There were no laws of decency observed or allowed; anything went, including sodomy, incest, and homosexuality. The Devil, with his scaly and cold sexual organ, had intercourse with as many of the witches as time would permit. But even so, he did display some discrimination: one young witch, in her confession, recalled that he took the pretty witches from the front, the ugly ones from behind. The orgy went on until the sound of the crowing cock could be heard, at which time the sated, debauched revelers disbanded, going their separate ways until the next sabbat should be convened.

ALL HALLOWS' EVE

*I*f there was one night of the year when witches were sure to be out and about, it was All Hallows' Eve or, as we know it today, Halloween. On this, the night before All Saints' Day (November 1), the witches were joined by every other member of the unholy crew — goblins and ghosts, demons and fairies — in midnight revels and devilry. It was also the night when the souls of the dead reputedly walked the earth, seeking the warmth of their family hearth once more before the desolate winter set in. Food and drink were put out for the lonely ghosts, who passed by to the west always, the direction of the setting sun. For the ancient Celts, All Hallows' Eve was the first night of the new year.

But all over Europe, it became customary to light bonfires on October 31 to mark the passage from autumn to winter, and to signal the coming of the cold and dark. The herds of livestock, which had roamed the fields and pastures all summer, were brought in to the barns and stalls, there to weather the snow and ice. Perhaps the bonfires were meant, symbolically, to shed their heat over all living creatures during the difficult months to come.

In many parts of the British Isles, boys would go from house to house, collecting a peat (a clump of dried sod) from every farmer and villager, with the words, "Give us a peat to burn the witches." When they had collected enough, they would stack them up with dry wood and straw and set fire to the pile. While it burned, they danced around it, shouting and playing games. But when the last sparks died down, and the darkness once again threatened to overwhelm them, the boys would cry out, "Devil take the hindmost!" and run for their very lives. It's possible that at one time the hindmost — the last to flee — was in fact made a human sacrifice.

In Ireland, All Hallows' Eve was known as the night the fairy folk moved their colonies from one hill to another, accompanied by the eerie sound of their tinkling bells and elf-horns. According to one old Irish story, a young man who stayed out late on one such night met up with a troop of the tiny people. At first they seemed like the perfect hosts, offering him a merry welcome, wine, and fairy gold. But when he took a closer look at them, he saw that they weren't fairies at all anymore; now they were the ghosts of neighbors who had died many years before. Terrified, he tried to run, but the ghosts grabbed hold of him and forced him into their antic dance. He fought to pry their fingers loose, but soon lost his strength and fell in a faint. When he awoke the next day, he was lying inside a stone circle, his arms bruised and sore from the grip of the fairy fingers.

FAMILIARS

"The witches have their spirits, some hath one, some hath
more, as two, three, four, or five, some in one likeness and
some in another, as like cats, weasels, toads, or mice,
whom they nourish with milk or a chicken, or by letting
them suck now and then a drop of blood."

George Gifford,
Dialogue Concerning Witches (1593)

The spirits that Gifford, a prominent English preacher, is speaking
of here were called familiars, and they were thought to be gifts from
Satan to his willing followers, the witches. They were given, the way one
might give a wedding present, to celebrate the consummation of the
witch's pact with the Devil.

Lowly demons, these familiars, it was said, did their best to fit unob-
trusively into the everyday world. To do so, they assumed all sorts of
animal shapes, everything from dogs to spiders, though black cats were,
of course, one of the most popular forms. Toads and frogs, because they
were cold-blooded, were also likely familiars. So were blackbirds and

crows, since they were thought to be birds of augury. But virtually any creature could do, and in witch trials everything from hedgehogs to bumblebees were cited as evidence.

But whatever shape they took, these familiars provided the witch with a range of services, from running malicious errands to offering advice on the Black Arts. In 1662, Isobel Gowdie, a Scottish witch, declared that "each of us has a spirit to wait upon us, when we please to call upon him." The familiars also served as a kind of social secretary, reminding the witches of the time and place for the next sabbat. Sometimes, witches were reported to ride these very familiars to the meeting place.

The feeding of the familiar was an economical, if unappetizing, act. As with imps (with whom they are somewhat interchangeable), familiars were nursed on the witch's milk, or blood; this they sucked from the witch's teat — generally a supernumerary nipple, which can appear on the bodies of men or women. This teat, or pap, was called the witch's mark.

THE WITCH'S MARK

In witch trials, there were two pieces of proof necessary for conviction: one was the familiar, and the other was the witch's mark. Neither one was very hard to find. The familiar, as has been mentioned above, could be a beloved pet, or a beetle scuttling across the floor of the witch's

The Witch-Finder General

hovel. The witch's mark could be anything from the supernumerary nipple — which would have been considered incontrovertible proof — to something as small as a mole, a wart, or other small physical anomaly. Only an absolutely perfect body could have withstood this scrutiny (and then the perfection would itself have been considered proof of an unholy pact).

And the scrutiny, make no mistake, was intense. Suspected witches were routinely stripped naked, shaved from head to toe, and then carefully inspected, sometimes in a public courtroom, by any number of noted witch-finders; on occasion, they were tied to a chair throughout. Since the witch's mark was often thought to be well concealed, the examination was quite thorough, and often turned up the damning evidence in the "privy parts." Though cloaked in moral rectitude, the witch trials, quite undeniably, fed the sadistic and prurient drives first of the prosecutors, and then of the public at large.

TOOLS OF THE TRADE

*L*ike any craftsman — and after all, it wasn't called witch*craft* for nothing — the witch had her own set of tools. These she used to cast her spells, concoct her potions, and in one way or another ply her trade. Though methods and implements varied, there were certain fairly standard items which one witch, dropping in unannounced at another witch's cottage, could reasonably expect to find there.

There was, of course, the *broomstick,* or *bune wand* (as it was known to Scottish witches), which she employed for her nocturnal flights. In the earliest accounts of witchcraft, it was usually just a forked wand, or a wooden staff. Long-stalked plants, such as yellow ragwort and beanstalks, also came into use, though the broomstick eventually became the acknowledged mode of transport. In Reginald Scot's *Discoverie of Witchcraft*, published in 1584, Scot wrote that "at these magicall assemblies [the sabbats], the witches never fail to danse . . . and whiles they sing and danse, everie one hath a broome in hir hand, and holdeth it up aloft." What went into the brooms was important too: in the Wrye Forest area of Worcestershire, for instance, oak twigs were used for the brush part, hazel for the shaft, and birch for the binding, because all three of these trees were invested with magical meaning. (The oak was the king of the forest, the hazel symbolized wisdom, and the birch purification.)

Perhaps the second most essential and recognizable tool In the witch's kit was her *cauldron.* Even in ancient Greece, the witches were already putting the cauldron to use. When Medea, the witch of Colchis and priestess of Hecate, plotted the murder of King Pelias, it was her magic cauldron she used to complete the deed. When Macbeth approaches the three Weird Sisters in their dark cave, they are gathered around their boiling cauldron: "Double, double toil and trouble, Fire burn and cauldron bubble," they chant in unison. And into the pot they toss such potent ingredients as eye of newt, tongue of dog, lizard's leg, and tooth of wolf. Then they give Macbeth the good and the bad news about his future prospects.

The Druidic moon goddess, Cerridwen, used magical herbs to brew her Cauldron of Inspiration. The stew had to simmer for a year and a day, and at the end of that time it produced the Three Drops of Wisdom (or divine inspiration), the mystical Awen. Ever after, the cauldron was adopted by witches as their unofficial symbol. Its capacity to transform what it received (turning assorted ingredients into food, or medicine) made it representative of the feminine principle; the three legs it was supported on symbolized the triple moon goddess; and the four elements of life — water, fire, earth, and air — all went into or out of it. (Water filled the cauldron, fire boiled it, the herbs of the earth cooked inside it, and steam arose from the bubbling brew.)

The third necessary tool in any witch's toolbox was her *witch ball*, or *speculum*. Sometimes the speculum was a crystal ball, sometimes it was a magic mirror. A witch short of funds could fashion one from a black bowl filled with water. Whatever she made it from, her witch ball was what she used for scrying, or divining things. Gazing into its reflective depths, she could see beyond the borders of time and space. She could predict future events, envision far-off places, and get answers to questions that continued to plague her ("Mirror, mirror, on the wall, Who's the fairest of them all?").

In seacoast towns, witches were known to employ the glass globes that fishermen used to keep their nets afloat. These were generally made of dark green or blue glass, and had the added advantage of appearing to be quite innocent objects. The well-known Irish witch, Biddy Early, had a favorite blue glass bottle.

Specula of any sort had to be consecrated before they were put to use, and this had to be done by exposing them to the light of a full moon. When not in use, they were generally kept in a closed box, or under a black velvet cloth. No matter what, they were kept out of the sun.

Exposing them to candlelight, however, was fine, and sometimes recommended. Some witches liked a candle to provide a fine pinpoint of light in the speculum while others preferred only a dimly diffused light in the room. Burning incense was a nice added touch. If all went well, the witch ball would eventually cloud over, and then the scryer would see misty pictures emerge. If she looked even harder, the pictures would become clearer and more brightly lit, and show her what she wanted to know. Sometimes this message could be quite literal — the face of the fairest person in the land — and sometimes it could be figurative, a sign or symbol that had to be interpreted. But for most witches, this was no problem; they were very good at deciphering puzzles.

Finally, no witch's arsenal was complete without a special knife. It wasn't used for such mundane purposes as chopping herbs. This dagger — black-handled, and inscribed on the blade with magical symbols —

was called her *Athame*. Traditionally given to a new witch on the night of her initiation, kind of like a sorority pin, the Athame was used for such mystical purposes as drawing the magic circle, mixing the sacred salt and water at the Esbat (the monthly meeting of a witches' coven), and controlling spirits that had been called down to Earth. A woodcut in a 1555 edition of a book called *History of the Northern Peoples* shows a witch acting like a ringmaster to a horde of boisterous demons. In one hand she holds aloft a sheaf of magical herbs, and in the other her gleaming Athame.

THE ELEMENTALS

*W*henever a coven of witches met, the high priestess, stretching out her arms, stood at each of the four points of the compass in turn. At each point, with her Athame drawn, she invoked the "Mighty One," or *Elemental,* that corresponded to that particular direction: earth for the north, air for the east, fire for the south, and water for the west. It was once thought that the universe had been created of these four Elementals, and by harnessing their powers the witches hoped to give power to their charms.

The Elementals themselves were thought to be neither human nor strictly spirit, but something in between. And there were untold numbers of each category. They could be conjured, they moved with the rapidity of spirits, but they were composed of flesh and blood and bone. They were not immortal — they could fall victim to disease and die — but they could never be imprisoned. In some ways they behaved like mortals — walking, talking, sleeping — but they could exist only in their own element. And there was a name and a distinct character profile ascribed to each one.

According to the alchemist Paracelsus, who systematized much of the Elemental lore, the Elementals who lived in the earth were dwarfish spirits who lurked underground, guarding hoards of secret treasure. Known as *gnomes,* they could also, if provoked, swell up like giants. And they harbored a certain malevolence toward man. Still, if a man was determined to keep a gnome as a servant, he could keep him in line: "If you do your duty to him," Paracelsus asserted, "he will do his duty to you."

The Elementals of the Air, however, were much friendlier and easier to handle. Known as *sylphs* or *sylvestres,* these airy sprites were the ones that most resembled humans.

In the water, the *undines* held sway. But they have also been known, unlike their fellow spirits, to marry mortals. If a man should happen to marry one, Paracelsus warned, he should be careful never to anger her while they were passing by a body of water: she could decide to jump in and disappear.

And *salamanders* were the Elementals of fire, named for the mythical lizardlike creatures that could live and breathe inside a bed of flames. No man could get too close to them, nor could they come too close to man. In his memoirs, Benvenuto Cellini claimed to have seen one in his family's fireplace, "sporting in the core of the intensest coals."

What the Elementals shared, in Paracelsus's view, was a distaste for drunkards and louts and people with too high an opinion of themselves. They liked, on the other hand, "natural men, who are simple-minded and child-like, innocent and sincere, and the less vanity and hypocrisy there is in a man, the easier it will be for him to approach them."

MAGICAL DEVICES

*E*very witch who could write kept a little book, and in it she recorded the recipes for her potions, the correct wording of her incantations, the results of her work. For the witch, this *Book of Shadows,* as it has come to be known, was the equivalent of a ship's log, or a scientist's lab book.

But in the days when witchcraft was a capital offense, such books were dangerous to keep. They were kept hidden, and upon the witch's death her fellows in the coven were instructed to take what they wanted from it, and then burn the original (as, indeed, its author may already have been burned).

Still, from what records and books do remain, there appear to have been certain tried and true means used by witches to achieve their magical ends.

Witches' brew.

Of the many potent charms regularly employed, one of the most popular was known as the *Hand of Glory*.

The recipe was fairly simple. A hand cut from the body of a hanged man was first wrapped in a piece of shroud, then the shroud cloth was drawn tight to squeeze out any blood that might still remain. The hand was next marinated, as it were, in an earthenware pot filled with salt, saltpeter, and peppers. Two weeks later, the hand was taken out of the pot and dried to a crisp — in the sun or, if time was of the essence, in an oven with vervain and fern.

What was the Hand of Glory good for? It was a kind of all-purpose charm. You lit the fingers and while it burned you could pursue whatever nefarious scheme you chose. According to Martin Del Rio, the sixteenth-century Jesuit demonologist, a thief once lit the Hand of Glory to keep the residents of a house asleep while he went through the drawers. To his misfortune, a servant girl saw him light it, and after several unsuccessful attempts to put it out by blowing on it, dousing it with water, then beer — she finally managed it with a pitcher of milk. (Why that worked remains a mystery.) The owners of the house instantly woke up, the burglar was caught, and the servant girl was rewarded for her valor.

Cautious homeowners could defend themselves against the Hand of Glory through the use of a special ointment. This ointment, according to *Marvellous Secrets of the Natural and Cabalistic Magic of Little Albert* (published in Cologne in 1772), had to be prepared in the dog days from three particular ingredients — the gall of a black cat, the blood of a screech owl, and the fat of a white hen. Smeared over the threshold of the house and all other entry points, it would keep any one from using the Hand of Glory to bewitch the house's inhabitants.

The *Witch's Ladder* was another homemade charm, though this one was somewhat easier to manufacture. All it required was a length of new rope or strong thread, and a clutch of white goose feathers. (Black feathers from a crow or rook were also sometimes used.)

While the strands of the rope or thread were being braided, the witch recited a malediction against the person she intended to do harm. She recited the curse every time she made a knot in the rope, and every time she made a knot she inserted a feather. When the job was done, she hid the bad luck charm in the victim's bed. By one account, it was also possible to weight the rope with a stone and sink it in a pond. As the bubbles rose to the surface, the power of the curse would be freed.

It was important that the rope have three strands — a magical number — and that the feathers come from a male bird. The feathers, it was thought, assured the witch that the curse would fly toward its target. In Italy, the charm was known as *la guirlanda delle streghe,* or *the witch's garland.*

The *Bellarmine Jug* got its name from Cardinal Bellarmine, whose scowling, bearded face often adorned it. Manufactured in the Rhineland from the 1500s on, the jugs were exported to England by the crateload and became a very popular household item.

But their uses weren't always benign.

A stout, stoneware vessel with a bulging body and a narrow neck, the Bellarmine Jug could be easily stoppered with a bit of cork. It could be used to hold anything from wine to honey, but it could also be used to hold the motley items needed to inflict or counteract a curse: as a result, it acquired the nickname of "witch bottle."

Witches wishing to inflict harm on someone could fill the Bellarmine Jug with the nail parings, the hair, and the urine of their intended victim. (In the days of chamberpots, it wasn't actually that difficult to get the urine sample.) Sometimes a scrap of red cloth was cut in the shape of a heart, then pierced with pins, and put inside, too. Once the jug was sealed again, it was buried in some secret spot or hurled into a river. Then it was considered just a matter of time before the victim began to sicken and fail.

The Bellarmine Jug was also often used as a defensive measure. If someone thought he had been cursed, he could procure the same personal items from his presumed nemesis and make his own witch bottle. Then, at midnight, while reciting the Lord's Prayer backwards, he could put the witch bottle in the fire to boil. The witch, it was thought, would feel her blood boil in the same way, and knowing that her curse had been thrown back at her she would quickly move to lift it. If the bottle exploded (which must have been particularly unpleasant) it was assumed that the witch had died.

The custom of the witch bottle has been around for many years. As late as the 1850s, a famous English herbalist and astrologer known as James ("Cunning") Murrell was using them in his country practice. Murrell lived in a little weatherboard cottage across a narrow lane from the Hadleigh Church. One day a girl showed up there in uncontrollable hysterics, scrambling on all fours, barking furiously like a dog. Her family suspected it was a gypsy's curse at work because earlier in the day, the girl had found a gypsy woman in the barn, and ordered her out. The woman had gone, but not before muttering, "You'll be sorry for this, my girl." That's when the fits had begun.

Murrell concurred with the family's diagnosis. He immediately prepared a witch bottle, filling it with herbs, pins, and samples of the girl's own urine and blood. (Although using the girl's own fluids was unusual, it was not unheard of.) Then he put the bottle on the fire to boil. The room was darkened, the doors locked, and everyone present was enjoined to keep perfect silence or the counterspell would not work.

A short while later, as they sat silently around the fire, they heard footsteps approaching the door, then loud and persistent knocking. An old woman cried out, "For God's sake, stop! You're killing me!" A second later the bottle burst, and the woman's voice died away. The girl's fits abated.

The next day, on a roadside three miles away, the half-burnt body of the gypsy woman was discovered by a passing traveler.

THE WITCH HUNT

*T*hough the words "witch" and "witchcraft" had already been in use for well over a thousand years, and its practices employed in countries all over the world, it was chiefly in western Europe, between 1450 and 1750, that the witch mania — and such it was — reached its terrible peak. It was then that the churches, Catholic and Protestant both, declared war on witches and raised them to a previously unheard-of prominence. It was then, too, that the churches led their adherents in what might be described as a massive pogrom, a roundup of these witches that resulted in unimaginable horrors and grisly executions. By some accounts, up to 200,000 people — mostly women — were tried, found guilty, and either hanged from the gallows or burned at the stake. (As a special mercy, those scheduled for burning were sometimes strangled first.) It was a mass hysteria and persecution seldom rivaled in human history.

Who were its victims? Chiefly, they were the women who had always concocted charms and folk remedies and herbal brews — many of which had genuine medicinal properties — and who had passed such secrets along. They were women who had the added misfortunes of living alone, of having a pet, of being old, poor, unattractive, and possibly a bit addled. These women ran the greatest risk of being charged with witchcraft, and could call on the fewest resources in their own defense.

But even youth and beauty were no protection: in 1629, a nineteen-year-old girl, Barbara Gobel, was burned at the stake; the executioner's list describes her as "the fairest maid in Wurzburg." Not far off, another young woman who went to the stake was called the "fairest and the purest maiden in all Cologne." Sometimes it was their very youth, beauty, and even piety which attracted the attention of the eager demonologists; these virtues, it was assumed, were just a clever disguise, Satan's way of concealing his followers among the innocent flock. But the witch-finders were not to be so easily fooled.

Clearly, there was no guarantee of safety for anyone.

Consequently, the persecutions went on and on and on. . .

THE LEGAL ARMORY

*W*itchcraft being a difficult charge to verify in court, judges and prosecutors were always happy to have any authoritative help they could get. For many years two books, weighty with erudition and freewheeling with their suggestions, provided them with all the ammunition they needed.

One was *De La Demonomanie des Sorciers* (or, *Of the Demonomania of Witches*). Written by a French lawyer and demonologist named Jean Bodin, the book was first published in Paris in 1580, though it appeared in numerous editions and translations thereafter. Bodin had served as a judge in many witchcraft trials, and in the *Demonomanie* he gathered together all that he had learned. Among other things, Bodin offered one of the first legal definitions of a witch: "One who knowing God's laws tries to bring about some act through an agreement with the Devil."

A particularly callous work, the *Demonomanie* provided plenty of tips for eager prosecutors. "One must not adhere to the ordinary rules of prosecution," Bodin advised, for "proof of such evil is so obscure and difficult that not one out of a million witches would be accused or punished, if regular legal procedure were followed." Consequently, Bodin recommended a number of questionable courtroom measures: the names of informers were never to be told, children were to be forced to indict their parents, suspicion of witchcraft was enough to warrant torture ("for popular rumor is almost never misinformed"), and "a person once accused should never be acquitted, unless the falsity of the accuser is clearer than the sun."

Bodin came down equally hard on the sentencing issue. All in favor of gruesome executions, he worried nonetheless that witches were often getting off too lightly: "Whatever punishment one can order against witches by roasting and cooking them over a slow fire is not really very much, and not as bad as the torment which Satan has made for them in this world, to say nothing of the eternal agonies which are prepared for them in hell, for the fire here cannot last more than an hour or so until the witches have died."

Any judge who failed to dispatch a convicted witch should, in Bodin's view, be executed himself.

The other book much loved by witch-hunters, and once described as "a perfect armory of judicial murder," was known as the *Malleus Maleficarum* (or *The Witches' Hammer*), first published in 1486. Bodin took much of his own information and zeal from its pages. Written in Latin by two Dominican friars, Jakob Sprenger, the Dean of Cologne University, and Prior Heinrich Kramer, the book was a virtual bible of witchcraft practice and lore. It was also one of the first international best-sellers, going into no less than thirteen editions before 1520, and sixteen more between 1574 and 1669. There were translations in German, French, English, and Italian.

The book was divided into three parts. The first part exhorted civil and ecclesiastical authorities to recognize the enormous scope of witchcraft — the number of its adherents, and the abominations they performed. It described in rambling, lurid detail how they renounced the Catholic faith, paid homage to Satan, cavorted with incubi and succubi. It also pointed out that to have any doubts about the existence of witches was in itself heretical: in Exodus 22:18, the Bible said, "Thou shalt not suffer a witch to live." What more instruction could you ask than that?

The second part was an intensive study of the various kinds of *maleficia* witches could do. Maleficia covered all the injuries and misfortunes that could befall mankind — from crop failures to heart attacks — and for which no other obvious cause was apparent; such trouble was assumed to be the malice of witches at work in the world.

In the final portion, the book got down to cases — literally. It explained how to start a legal action against a witch, how to gather evidence, and how to extract that all-important confession: technically speaking, a witch could not be condemned without one. But as the text (a quarter million words, all told) also offered lots of tips on interrogation, imprisonment and torture, the confession was never that difficult to come by.

This last part of the *Malleus Maleficarum* has one other distinction; it appears to be chiefly the work of only one of the authors, Heinrich Kramer, who had had plenty of experience in the pursuit and prosecution of witches. He had spearheaded the effort in the Tyrol, and he'd done it with such ferocity that even the Tyroleans had rebelled against him. At one point, to bolster his case, he'd hired a local woman (of easy virtue and meager means) to hide in an oven and pretend to be the

Devil; from inside, she denounced many of the local townspeople. Kramer had then rounded them up and put them through the most extreme forms of torture. The Bishop of Blixen, after much struggle, eventually succeeded in expelling him from the region. But Kramer was a busy man; in 1484, he procured from Innocent VIII a papal bull silencing opposition to witch hunts. And with the publication of the *Malleus Maleficarum,* he restored himself to pride of place as witch expert extraordinaire.

INTERROGATION

*W*hen witch trials were at their height, during the sixteenth and seventeenth centuries, the interrogation of suspected witches became so routine that in many regions a set list of questions was developed that could be used quickly and uniformly. The judges of Colmar in Alsace, for instance, arrived at twenty-nine in all, which they labeled: *Questions to Be Asked of a Witch:*

1. How long have you been a witch?
2. Why did you become a witch?
3. How did you become a witch, and what happened on that occasion?

4. Who is the one you chose to be your incubus? What was his name?
5. What was the name of your master among the evil demons?
6. What was the oath you were forced to render him?
7. How did you make this oath, and what were its conditions?
8. What finger were you forced to raise? Where did you consummate your union with your incubus?
9. What demons and what other humans participated at the sabbat?
10. What food did you eat there?
11. How was the sabbat banquet arranged?
12. Were you seated at the banquet?
13. What music was played there, and what dances did you dance?
14. What did your incubus give you for your intercourse?
15. What devil's mark did your incubus make on your body?
16. What injury have you done to such and such a person, and how did you do it?
17. Why did you inflict this injury?
18. How can you relieve this injury?
19. What herbs or what other methods can you use to cure these injuries?
20. Who are the children on whom you have cast a spell? And why have you done it?
21. What animals have you bewitched to sickness or death, and why did you commit such acts?

22. Who are your accomplices in evil?
23. Why does the devil give you blows in the night?
24. What is the ointment with which you rub your broomstick made of?
25. How are you able to fly through the air? What magic words do you utter then?
26. What tempests have you raised, and who helped you to produce them?
27. What [plagues of] vermin and caterpillars have you created?
28. What do you make these pernicious creatures out of and how do you do it?
29. Has the devil assigned a limit to the duration of your evildoing?

Considering that witches were questioned under torture, and that failing to reply just increased the punishment, it's not surprising that there were many confessions. The victim's replies were sometimes entered in court records with a simple "affirmat" (admitted); at other times, a scribe prepared what was called a *relatio,* a kind of public summary of what happened in court, including, most notably, the witch's full confession. Written in the first person, as if the witch were simply telling her story of her own volition, these confessions had to be signed by the witch herself, and were generally read aloud to the crowd that assembled later on for the execution.

TESTING, TESTING

*I*n trials for witchcraft, a thousand different stratagems were used to ferret out the guilt of the accused and elicit that all-important confession. If the usual methods of torture didn't work — and they seldom failed — there were other tests that the prosecutors could employ.

One of the oldest, revived in the twelfth century from a far earlier time, was the *bier right.*

The ritual itself was fairly simple: the body of a murder victim was laid out, and the accused was brought toward it. If the body bled anew, then that was all the proof needed. In the view of many noted demonologists, the hatred that the murder victim felt for the murderer remained in the body somehow, and the approach of the murderer made the victim's blood surge once more.

In the Dalkeith witch trial of 1661, a woman named Christine Wilson was accused of murder but claimed she was innocent. The bier right was invoked by the court. Wilson, according to a manuscript in Scotland's National Museum of Antiquities, "refused to come nigh the corpse or to touch it, saying that she never touched a dead corpse in her life. But being earnestly desired by the minister and bailiffs . . . that she

---

would but touch the corpse softly, she granted to do it . . . she touching the wound of the dead man very softly, it being white and clean without any spot of blood or the like, yet immediately, while her finger was upon it, the blood rushed out of it to the great admiration of all the beholders, who took it as a discovery of the murderer."

Swimming the witch was another method of ascertaining guilt, though this one could prove fatal regardless of the outcome. The reputed witch was first elaborately tied, her right thumb to her left big toe, and vice versa, so that she was "cross bound": then, while loosely roped to men on shore, she was thrown into deep water to see if she would sink. If she did (and sometimes drowned in the process), she was declared innocent. But if she managed to stay afloat, she was determined to be a witch. The rationale? It was the considered opinion of no less a figure than King James I of England, as expressed in his *Daemonologie* (1597), that witches, having "shaken off them the sacred water of baptism and willfully refused the benefit thereof," would be rejected — that is, made to float on the surface — of any body of water they were ducked in.

Witches were also presumed to be preternaturally light (allowing one more reason for why they might float). By this same reasoning, they were occasionally weighed against the big Bible in the parish church. But this test was not used as often as others, perhaps because too many suspected witches managed to pass it.

THE WITCH-FINDER GENERAL

*M*atthew Hopkins, the self-proclaimed Witch-Finder General, had methods of his own for the discovery of witchcraft, including what he claimed to be a secret list containing the names of all those who had made such a pact with the Devil. This list, of course, was never seen by anyone but himself.

Armed with it, Hopkins launched in 1645 a bloody purge of witches throughout the eastern counties of England; before he was stopped, he had sent hundreds of people to the stake and the gallows, making himself, not incidentally, a wealthy man along the way.

The son of a minister, Hopkins took up the law. Despite being ruthless and utterly unscrupulous by nature, his practice in Ipswich mysteriously failed to thrive. He knew he had to find some other line of work, and it was while he was casting around for the right opportunity that the witch craze began to seize the Puritan areas of England. Recognizing his chance, Hopkins quickly read a few books on the subject — including *Daemonologie* by James I, Potts's account of the Lancashire witches, and Richard Bernard's *Guide to Grand Jurymen* — and then hung out his shingle as Witch-Finder General. For a price (at first a pound per head) he claimed to be able to root out and exterminate the witches in any city or village. And in only a few months' time, he had more business than he knew what to do with.

His first big chance came when the wife of a tailor in the town of Manningtree fell ill, and the tailor became convinced that it was the work of a witch, a one-legged old woman named Elisabeth Clarke. Hopkins got wind of the charge and flew into town to lead the prosecution. He convinced the local magistrates that he should be allowed to keep the prisoner awake for several days and nights in a row, ostensibly to catch her familiars, or imps, when they came for their regular feeding. In fact, he simply wanted to torture Clarke through sleep deprivation. After a few days, during which Hopkins and his cronies claimed to have witnessed the visitations of a whole range of familiars, including a kitten, two dogs, a hare, a toad, and a polecat, the old woman, exhausted and confused, made a full confession. When questioned about her accomplices, she gave the name of another old woman, Anne West.

Now Hopkins was on a roll. He arrested Anne West, and remarkably, the woman's own daughter, Rebecca, confirmed that her mother was a witch. Rebecca went on to tell stories about other local women, too, who she said read from a book of incantations, prayed to the Devil, and sent their imps — two dogs and two kittens — to do harm to both cattle and humans all over the district. Hopkins rounded up the others, and before leaving town he had succeeded in having six of the women, including Clarke and Anne West, hanged. The daughter, who admitted that she too had had carnal relations with the Devil, was for unknown reasons spared.

Hopkins's authority was now established, and with a team of professional "prickers" — experts who claimed to be able, with long needles, to find the insensible spot on a witch's body where the Devil had set his seal — he started traveling from town to town, quickly setting up shop, and after summary trials executing anywhere from one to dozens of witches. He was paid a generous fee by each village he visited, in large part determined by the number of witches he was able to deliver to the gallows. In Suffolk alone, he arrested 124 people on charges of witchcraft, and no less than 68 of them were executed.

And though most of the victims were elderly and impoverished women, men were suspect, too. In one case, a seventy-year-old clergyman, John Lowes, was arrested. His parish in Brandeston had grown weary of him, and when he refused to give up his post voluntarily, the congregation charged him with being a witch. Hopkins had him "swum" in the castle moat, then dragged him out and forced him to march back and forth across a room until, collapsing in exhaustion, he confessed to being a wizard. Among other things, he volunteered that he had sent a yellow imp to sink a ship at sea, with the loss of 14 lives. Denied the traditional church rites, Lowes had to recite his own burial service on his way to the town gallows.

As Hopkins's persecutions grew larger, wider, and ever more bloody, an opposition slowly began to form. A Parliamentary Commission was established that endorsed witch hunts but ruled out "swimming," one of Hopkins's favorite tortures. A prominent vicar, the Rev. John Gaule of Great Staughton, attacked him from the pulpit, and published an indictment of his brutal methods in a tract called *Select Cases of Conscience Touching Witches and Witchcraft.* Hopkins attempted to answer Gaule's charges in a pamphlet of his own, *The Discovery of Witchcraft,* but the tide had begun to turn against him — and he knew it. Taking his ill-gotten gains, Hopkins quietly retired to his home in Manningtree, where he died in his bed, of tuberculosis, in 1647.

APPARITIONS

"From ghoulies and ghosties and
Long-leggety beasties
And things that go bump in the night,
Good Lord, deliver us!"

Scottish prayer

HARBINGERS OF DEATH

*I*n every culture and in every land there were superstitions, signs, omens that foretold the coming of death. One, for instance, was the clock that stopped, or chimed unexpectedly between the hours; the disturbance in this normal marking of time signaled that Death was keeping an eye on the house. So, too, an ordinary candle could send a message; if the melting wax slid down the shaft in a broad sheet, like a shroud, a death was imminent. And birds were often considered harbingers of doom, or psychopomps, sent to convey a spirit from this world to the next. If a bird flew in through an open window, or beat his wings against a closed shutter; if an owl hooted ceaselessly nearby; if a raven deserted its flock and cawed beside the door—all of these were unhappy portents for anyone living within.

There were also ghostly figures that haunted the world, roaming the fields, the forests, the village streets, waiting to deliver their own dreaded news. And for a mortal, just setting eyes on one of these was oftentimes enough to call forth calamity.

The Ankou

In Brittany, a part of western France, a fearful spectre known as the Ankou traveled the roads at night, plodding along beside a creaking cart, pulled by a team of skeletal horses. Those inside a house or tavern could sometimes hear the rattling of the cart as it slowly passed by, and they were careful not even to peer outside, lest they catch the attention of the Ankou himself. To do so was surely to die.

Tall and haggard, with long white hair, wearing black clothes and the broad-brimmed hat of the Breton farmer, the Ankou carried a scythe, honed on a human bone, over one shoulder. He walked with the stiff gait of the blind — his eye sockets empty — twisting his head and sniffing the air for those foolish enough to have ignored the curfew bells. Who he was exactly remained unclear. By some accounts, he was Cain, the first man to have killed his brother, now doomed to wander the Earth for eternity, gathering up the other human dead. By other accounts, he was the ghost of the last man to have died in the previous year, returning to find new companions in the cold ground where he now lay. By all accounts, he was, in effect, the Reaper.

Most terrifying of all was to encounter the Ankou on the roads anytime between dusk and the hour just before dawn. Anyone caught unawares would be struck from behind and knocked face-first into the ground; the dirt they tasted then was like the dirt that would be flung on the lid of their coffin, within two years at the most. Those who met up with the Ankou very late at night were even less fortunate; they would be claimed within the month — their bodies, along with so many others, thrown into the wooden cart that was, miraculously, never filled.

BLACK SHUCK

He had many names, in many different parts of the British Isles — in Norfolk he was Black Shuck, in Suffolk the Galley Trot, in Lancashire Shriker, in Yorkshire Padfoot. But the descriptions were always the same — a huge shaggy dog, black as night, with saucerlike eyes that glowed red in the dark. A descendant, it is thought, of the hound of Odin (the Norse god of war), the spectral hound was seen on the coasts, the midlands, the fens and moors. Often he was seen prowling the country roads at night, looking for unlucky travelers who should have been home for the night. Those who saw him coming, and whom the dog saw in turn, he would fix with his baleful stare as he swelled up to the size of a calf before disappearing again into the darkness. But just to have seen him was more than enough: that traveler's days were numbered, and few.

THE WILD HUNT

Sometimes the dog was not one, but many, and sometimes the pack of baying hounds was accompanied by a pack of spectral riders led by the Devil himself. Feared throughout northern Europe, the Wild Hunt took place on stormy midwinter nights, when the Devil enjoyed a midnight ride.

For company, he kept the souls of the tormented dead, who rode with him to fetch the souls of those still living. The yelping hounds were demons, or in some accounts the spirits of unbaptized children. The hunters would gallop through the air, horns blaring, spurs jangling, and anyone they found abroad and unprotected they swept up and transported to some far distant place, to be left, abandoned and lost. The only hope for anyone who heard them coming was to fall face-down on the ground and cling for dear life to any bush or branch in reach. Looking up was ill advised; the Devil could inflict instant death, madness, or any of a host of other misfortunes on anyone who caught his eye.

There were many stories to prove the point. According to one, a farmer was once returning late from the Widecombe Fair in Devon, and he wasn't making much progress. For one thing, he'd had too much ale, and for another the night had turned stormy and cold. With his hat pulled down, and his horse barely able to find the trail, he was plodding along through the wind and rain when his horse suddenly stopped altogether.

The farmer looked up from under his hat and saw a pack of hounds dancing around the horse's hooves. Just ahead of him was a coal-black horse, with a huntsman all in black mounted in the saddle; the hunter's face was concealed by a broad-brimmed hat. Slung across his saddle were the carcasses of whatever he'd killed.

The farmer, still feeling the effects of the ale, laughed and said, "Huntsman, share your spoils," and the huntsman, glancing down, laughed too. He lifted one of the parcels off his saddle, tossed it at the farmer, then abruptly turned his horse and rode off into the darkness.

The farmer ripped the covering away from the parcel, then nearly fell from his own horse in shock. What he thought he saw there, in the brief flash of lightning from overhead, was the body of his own young son. But a second later, when he wiped the rain from his eyes and looked again, all he saw there were his own shaking hands.

Suddenly sobered, he dug his heels into the flanks of his mare and galloped the rest of the way home. He had no sooner dismounted than his wife, wailing, emerged at the door, holding in her arms the lifeless body of their infant son.

The Banshee

In Scotland and Ireland, mortals had another strange vision to fear: the banshee (or "fairy woman"), who haunted remote streams and secret pools. There, she knelt by the water, endlessly beating blood-stained shrouds against the stones, wringing them dry, and singing to herself a mournful dirge. If a traveler was brave enough to speak to her, she would tell him the names of those who were soon to die — it was their shrouds she was washing — and if he insisted, she would tell him his own fate, too.

According to legend, the banshee, in life, had been a young woman who had died before her time in childbirth. She would go on laundering the shrouds of those who were soon to join her until the day came when she would have died a natural death herself. By other accounts, the banshee was the ghost of a family member, long deceased, who would appear when another member of the clan was about to die. Bony and white, with streaming hair and blood-red eyes, she would weep and wail outside the house at night. Her keening would pierce the very walls, and her face would appear at first one window and then the next. She was looking, it was said, for the one about to die, and when she found him or her, she would beckon. And the one to whom she had done so, the one who had seen the banshee crook her fleshless finger, had no choice but to follow.

Nor was moving the clan to far-off shores any assurance of escaping the banshee. In her book on the ancient legends of Ireland, Lady Wilde (Oscar's mother) recounted the story of the O'Grady family, who traveled to Canada, away from the "mysterious influences of the old land of their forefathers." If they had hoped to escape "the spirit of death," they had not gone far enough; the Ban-Sidhe, as Lady Wilde spelled it, had apparently tracked them across the seas:

> ". . . one night a strange and mournful lamentation was heard outside the house. No word was uttered, only a bitter cry, as of one in deepest agony and sorrow, floated through the air.
>
> Inquiry was made, but no one had been seen near the house at the time, though several persons distinctly heard the weird, unearthly cry, and a terror fell upon the household, as if some supernatural influence had overshadowed them.
>
> Next day it so happened that the gentleman and his eldest son went out boating. As they did not return, however, at the usual time for dinner, some alarm was excited, and messengers were sent down to the shore

to look for them. But no tidings came until, precisely at the exact hour of the night when the spirit-cry had been heard the previous evening, a crowd of men were seen approaching the house, bearing with them the dead bodies of the father and the son, who had both been drowned by the accidental upsetting of the boat, within sight of land, but not near enough for any help to reach them in time.

Thus the Ban-Sidhe had fulfilled her mission of doom, after which she disappeared, and the cry of the spirit of death was heard no more."

THE DOPPELGANGER

The frightful image seen at the window, or staring back from the mirror, could be your own — a double, or doppelganger (from the German for "double goer"), the sight of which could foretell your own imminent demise.

Sometimes described as the soul embodied, sometimes an astral projection or aura, the double most often presented itself as a warning. Queen Elizabeth I reportedly saw a vision of herself lying on her deathbed, pale and still, soon before she died. Goethe and Shelley also claimed to have seen their doubles, and when Catherine the Great of Russia saw her own coming toward her, she took no chances and ordered her soldiers to shoot at it.

Witches, it was long accepted, could project their own doubles and set them loose to do mischief far and wide. As a result, many a woman was hanged as a witch even though it could be proved beyond a shadow of a doubt that she was somewhere else entirely when the barn burned down, the cow died, or whatever else had happened that she was now charged with having done.

On other occasions, a double—of someone else—could be called forth or seen. One old Halloween custom has it that if a young girl lights two candles before a mirror, while eating an apple, she will see in the mirror the spectral image of her future husband, peering back at her as if from over her shoulder. If she is brave enough to venture out to a graveyard, and walk all the way around it twelve times, she will meet up with the double itself.

According to another old belief, anyone who wants to know who will pass away in the coming year has only to stand vigil near the church door on April 24, the eve of the feast day of St. Mark. At midnight, the airy doubles of all who will die file in a solemn processional into the church. If the watcher is unlucky enough to see his own image there, he knows his own time is not far off.

To this day, the fear of the double is observed, if unknowingly, in the custom of covering all the mirrors in a house where a death has just occurred. The double of anyone passing the glass, it was once thought, could be projected into the mirror and carried off by the deceased to the afterworld.

THE SHIVERING BOY

At Triermain Castle, in Northumberland, it is not so much a sight as a touch that is to be feared . . . the touch of tiny, icy fingers, and a little boy's voice whispering, "Cold, cold, forever more."

The boy, legend has it, lived in the fifteenth century, and had inherited the castle when his father died. The uncle who was made the boy's ward wanted the castle for himself, so he starved the boy until he was barely alive, then abandoned him on Thirwell Common in the midst of a winter storm. The boy perished in the snow.

But he returned to the castle in death, and walks the halls, teeth chattering, a spectral six-year-old shivering with the cold. If he enters the room of someone asleep, he may simply stand whimpering by the bed . . . or he may reach out and lay an ice-cold hand on the sleeper's brow. To feel his touch, or see his sad little figure, is a portent of trouble to come.

CORPSE CANDLES

They were fleeting lights, sometimes white, sometimes blue or green, moving mysteriously in the night. Often they were seen in church-yards, and often, too, in bogs or marshes. Because they hovered at the height of a candle held by what should have been a human hand (but wasn't), they were called, in Wales and some other countries, "corpse candles." To see them was to be forewarned of your own coming death.

These dancing balls of eerie light had many other names, too — will-o'-the-wisp, jack-o'-lantern, elf light, St. Elmo's fire (when seen at sea), friar's lantern, fetch light, and *ignis fatuus*, or "foolish fire." Even today, such lights are sometimes seen, but they are thought to be cre-ated by unusual atmospheric conditions, and the ignition of gases produced by the decay of plant or animal matter. In swamps, and for that matter old churchyards, such an explanation makes some sense. But it was not an explanation known to our ancestors. To them, the corpse candles were portents, or visitors from another world, here to do mischief in this one.

Stories abound of men and women foolish enough to track the beckoning flame. Travelers thinking it might be the light of a distant shelter followed it unknowingly into abysmal swamps, losing their way

Virgil surrounded by devils.

and falling into dense brush and treacherous waters. Germans thought the lights were the ghosts of those who had stolen land from their neighbors; Finns called them *liekkio* and believed they were the spirits of children who had been buried in the woods. In some northern European lands, the lights were thought to be the spirits of ancient warriors, still guarding the treasure that had been secreted in their burial mounds. But everyone agreed that following the lights was a dangerous and often deadly idea.

GHOSTS OF ICY CLIMES

*I*n Scandinavia and the northern countries of Europe, the full complement of spectral figures haunted the deep woods and valley towns. Lonely, sad, but unthreatening to mortals, these apparitions merely went their own way, traveling through the cold and dark on errands they would never in any lifetime complete. Among them were the ghosts of dead farmers, still trying in vain to perform their chores; the ghosts of poor elderly couples, who could be seen sitting together in the cottage where they had once lived, feeding peat to a fire that no longer burned; the ghosts of lovers, walking arm in arm from the churchyard at night.

But there were other ghosts, too, who were not so harmless, ghosts who displayed a peculiar malevolence toward the living, toward those who had wronged them, and anyone else who still drew breath. Among these spirits that roamed the arctic night were . . .

SENDINGS

According to the magical lore of Iceland, those skilled in the black arts could make their own ghosts — called sendings — out of human bones. These ghosts were expressly made to perform murder, and one particular story points up their terrible intent.

An attractive widow living on her own farmland was courted by many men in the village, but she wasn't interested in marrying any of them. All of them went their way except for one, a known wizard, who took her refusal hard.

On a warm afternoon, while the widow was preparing supper for her farmhands, she got an uneasy feeling. She was in the larder, and when she turned around she saw a black shadow, with a white spot at the center, creeping slowly across the wall. She knew it was a sending, and she stabbed it — in the white circle, the only vulnerable spot — with her kitchen knife. The knife instantly disappeared, and so did the shadow. It wasn't until the next morning when she went into the yard that she found the knife again — piercing a broken human bone.

GROUNDED GHOSTS

In Denmark, anyone who wandered into an open field or meadow was warned to keep an eye out for wooden stakes or posts driven into the ground. Ghosts that had been exorcised were pressed down into the earth and held there by a wooden stake driven through their heart. If a passerby happened to disturb the stake, the ghost, anxious to be released again, would whisper eagerly, "You pull, and I will push!"

Needless to say, it wasn't a good idea to heed these instructions.

THE NAVKY

As if travelers didn't have enough to fear from brigands and wild beasts, in Slavic lands they were also endangered by the spirits of children who had been murdered by their mothers, or died before baptism. Known as the *navky,* these spirits often took the shape of infants or young girls; rocking and weeping in the tree branches, they begged the travelers for baptism, or — if they were still angry at the living — tried to lure the travelers over cliffs, or into raging waters. In some lands, the navky were said to appear as great black birds whose loud cries could make the blood run cold.

THE UTBURD

In Norway, too, ghostly children assailed the living.

Infants who were born deformed, or sickly, or to a family that was simply incapable of feeding another mouth, were often abandoned. A rough grave was scraped in the snow, and the baby was left there to die of exposure. But that wasn't always the end of its life. When one of these tiny souls returned as a ghost, it was known as an *utburd* — from the old Norse word for "a child carried outside."

And though its earthly time had been short, this ghostly infant's wrath could be long and extraordinary.

Its vengeance was directed first at its own mother, and according to legend, it could drift beneath a door, through a crack in a window, or down a chimney, as nothing more than a wisp of smoke. Then it could take the shape of a frozen, withered child, and attack with uncanny strength.

But the utburd's rage extended to all mankind. It could maim or kill anyone unwise enough to pass by its tiny grave after dark. The cry it made was a lonely, mournful sound, and once it had set its sights on a victim, it could take on many different shapes and grow to immense

Lucifer preparing some new evil.

proportion. Any traveler who heard its call was advised to flee, and not even look back; the sight of the utburd was enough to freeze its quarry with terror. The ghost would come crashing out of the woods or down the road in hot pursuit. And the traveler had only two ways to save himself — by crossing a running stream, or producing something made of iron, usually a knife. If he could do neither, he would be grasped by the utburd, pulled to the ground, and crushed to pieces in its deadly embrace.

Denied such intimacy in life, the ghostly child took it in death.

THE POLTERGEIST

*I*f all the denizens of the spirit world could be considered as one large (and hopelessly dysfunctional) family, then the poltergeist would undoubtedly be the youngest son — bursting with energy, prone to mischief, and utterly beyond control.

Making one of its earliest appearances in the *Annales Fuldenses,* an ancient German manuscript, a poltergeist (German for "noisy spirit") is reported to have harassed a farmer near Bingen on the Rhine. First, it threw stones at his house, then it started to follow him around as he did his chores. Occasionally it set fire to something, and in an audible voice it denounced the poor man for his sins, and accused the village priest of indecent acts. Odd behavior though this may be, it is not uncommon procedure for the poltergeist.

Since then, poltergeists have made many and sundry appearances in the chronicles of the occult. In 1579, Girolamo Menghi wrote that a poltergeist had teased and annoyed a servant girl in Bologna, playing tricks on her and making rude noises. Peter Binsfeld, in 1589, said that a tenant should be allowed to break a lease if the premises were troubled by a poltergeist. And in his *Jardin de las Floras Curiosas* (1570), the Spanish writer Turrecremata told the story of a house in Salamanca where two beautiful young girls lived, along with a rollicking poltergeist. When the mayor and twenty men went to the house to rid it of its ghost, they were barraged with a hail of stones, and sent scurrying. When they renewed their attack, the stones flew again, but from no discernible hand. Finally, one of the men picked up one of the stones and threw it back inside the house, shouting, "If this came from you, O Devil, throw the same stone back at me." The stone came back, and the immediate consensus was that unnatural forces were indeed at work.

In general, poltergeists are more of a nuisance than a danger. They delight in playing pranks — throwing dishes off tables, emitting sulphurous smells, slamming doors, pulling blankets from the bed. They are drawn to families with young children, and if the family happens to be that of a minister, so much the better. (See "The Epworth Poltergeist," which follows.) They're also given to hiding things, which then turn up,

Beelzebub, Lord of the Flies.

after much searching, in the most unlikely places — an inkwell in the butter churn, a key ring in the hayloft. For any household beset by a poltergeist, it's a little like living with a hyperkinetic and invisible child — though sometimes, as with the family of the Reverend Wesley, they informally adopt it.

THE EPWORTH POLTERGEIST

The Epworth Rectory, located in an English market town, was the home of the Reverend Samuel Wesley, his wife, and their ten children. It was a large, happy household, undisturbed until a cold December night in 1716, when the servants were roused by a loud knock on the door and the sound of someone groaning outside. Thinking it might be Mr. Turpine, an ailing neighbor who sometimes stopped at the rectory, the servants opened the door. But it wasn't Mr. Turpine; indeed, it was no one at all. Puzzled, the servants went back to their tea, when the knocking came again — only much louder and more insistent this time. Again, they opened the door to find no one outside. The tea having lost some of its savor by now, the servants firmly bolted the door and decided to go to bed.

It was while the manservant was climbing the stairs, candle in hand, that he noticed his own shadow etched against the wall with a startling brightness. Then he heard a strange noise from the kitchen. Crouching down and peering through the balusters, he saw the iron hand mill, used to grind grain, grinding away on the kitchen table — but with no one turning its handle. Electing not to investigate any further, he raced up the stairs and jumped into bed.

From that night on, the Epworth rectory was bedeviled by the poltergeist. Sometimes it rattled the door latches and banged on the windows, sometimes it swept through a room with the sound of swishing petticoats, sometimes it gobbled like a turkey in the dark. The reverend himself tried to reason with it, asking it one night "what it was and why it disturbed innocent children and did not come to me in my study, if it had anything to say to me." The only reply he got was a knock on the outside of the house.

Mrs. Wesley had only slightly better luck. Tracking the noises to the nursery one day, she went inside, and the room immediately fell silent. But she felt that something was still in the room with her. On an impulse, she bent down to look under the bed of one of her daughters, and something small and swift —"much like a badger," as she wrote in one of her letters — scurried out, too fast for her to see or catch it.

Over the next several weeks, the family gradually grew so used to the poltergeist's shenanigans, and so weary of trying to exorcise it, that they gave it a name — "Old Jeffrey," after a previous tenant of the rectory who had died there — and learned to accommodate it in their daily schedule. Mrs. Wesley announced that she was under no circumstances to be disturbed between five and six o'clock, when she was offering her evening prayers — and the poltergeist obeyed. The children took to playing with it; as soon as it manifested itself in any particular part of the house, the children rushed at the spot, arms outstretched, hoping to grab it before it disappeared again.

Perhaps they eventually wore out even the ghost. A couple of months after it had rapped at the door, the poltergeist made its last audible appearance, just after the family had said its devotions. There were "two soft strokes," Wesley recorded, "at the morning prayers for King George, above stairs." And then, as unexpectedly as he had come, the Epworth Poltergeist — Old Jeffrey — went away. "As for the noises, etc. in our family," the reverend wrote, "I thank God we are now all quiet."

HOMEBODIES

𝒯hough ghosts have been known to appear almost anywhere, on mountain crags and tramp steamers, in coal mines and train stations, they show, like the poltergeist, a marked propensity for home. Sometimes it's because it was there they died — perhaps under violent circumstances — and they cannot leave, as it were, the scene of the crime. Sometimes it's because they feel compelled to reveal the mystery of their death to someone still living. And sometimes ghosts still haunt their homes because it was the only place they knew true happiness, and they cannot, even in death, tear themselves away. (The very word "haunt" originally meant "to fetch home.") There are a thousand such stories, of homebody ghosts, but those that follow make the point quite well.

House to Let

Inexpensive rentals have been sought after as long as there have been people seeking shelter, but exceptionally good deals have always been hard to come by. Even in ancient Athens.

The philosopher Athenodorus, on a visit there, came upon a large and impressive house, being offered for lease at a remarkably low rate. Wondering why, he made inquiries around the neighborhood and soon found out the reason: everyone who had tried to live there had been frightened away by the ghost of a filthy, skeletal man. Around his bony legs and arms the ghost wore clanking chains, caked with rust and dirt. One encounter with him, and most of the tenants were out the door.

But Athenodorus couldn't resist the challenge. He rented the place, then sat up late, waiting for the ghost. He was not disappointed. The spectre appeared, rattling his iron fetters, but Athenodorus stood his ground. The ghost then beckoned to him, as if to say, "Follow me." Athenodorus followed, and the ghost dragged his chains into the courtyard, where it stopped, turned, and suddenly disappeared.

Having marked the spot well, Athenodorus prevailed upon the city magistrates the next day to have the stones dug up, and the earth beneath them explored. There, according to the account given by Pliny the Younger, "they found bones, twisted round with chains, which were left bare and corroded by the fetters when time and the action of the soil had rotted away the body." The bones were gathered up and given a proper burial, and the ghost no longer haunted the house. (Though history does not record it, the landlord no doubt doubled the rent.)

THE GHOST OF
BURTON AGNES HALL

Anne Griffith, a young woman living in the reign of Elizabeth I, grew up in the great manor house of Burton Agnes Hall. It was there, in Yorkshire, that she played games with her sisters, received her suitors, came of age — and it was there, of an unknown disease, that she died young. On her deathbed, in the presence of the vicar, she made her sisters swear a solemn promise: her head, she said, was to be severed from her body and kept in the manor house always. Her sisters agreed to her strange request but, thinking she was mad with fever, did not honor it after her death. Her body, head still attached, was laid to rest beneath a bed of flowers in the family tomb.

For several days the house was quiet, steeped in mourning — until one night when the halls echoed with the sound of hollow grief and laughter. The men of the house piled out of bed, drew their swords, and searched everywhere for the source of the unearthly noise, but they could find nothing. Nor did they have any better luck the next night, when the terrifying screams, the agonized moans, began again. The whole house seemed to be filled with the doleful wailing, and at their wits' ends, the sisters hurried to the vicarage to see what could be done.

The vicar, remembering the deathbed request, advised the sisters to open the tomb. Reluctantly, they did so; with torches lighted, they descended into the cold stone vault, opened Anne's coffin, and to their horror found that the corpse had already begun their work for them: the head had separated itself from the body, shed itself of flesh, and was now propped upright on its jaws, empty eye sockets staring blankly. It all but asked to be taken inside. Dutifully, the sisters carried the skull back into the manor house with them and placed it with great care in the salon, in the center of the table. And for years, it stayed there, keeping a grisly watch on the doings of the now untroubled house.

The house might have remained untroubled, too, if it weren't for the attentions of a too fastidious scullery maid. Thinking that the awful thing had long since outlived its usefulness, she snatched it up one day and tossed it into the back of a passing cabbage cart. Instantly, the cart jolted to a stop, the driver nearly toppling from his seat. He checked his wheels, he lashed his horse, but nothing would make the cart move. Eventually, his cursing brought the master of the house outside to see what was causing all the ruckus.

It was then that the maid confessed to what she'd done. When the master demanded that she retrieve the skull, she blanched and swore she would not dare to touch the thing again. A young man, a member of the family, did the job for her — and the moment he did, the cart bolted forward. The skull was put back where it belonged, and order was once again restored to Burton Agnes Hall.

Many years later, the family of Anne Griffith gave up possession of the house, and a new family moved in. The first thing to go, of course, was that awful relic sitting on the salon table. A servant was told to bury it in the garden. But he had no sooner smoothed the dirt over it than the house shook again with the ghastly screams. All night long the new-comers shivered in their beds, held their hands over their ears, and probed the shadows for the source of the terrible sounds. In the morning, they found their horses had gone lame, and the garden was blackened by a late frost.

An old servant, one who knew the house and its legend well, took a spade and tromped out into the garden. He found the spot where the skull had been buried and dug it up again. Brushing the dirt away, he brought it back inside the manor house. Without asking anyone's leave, he put it back in its accustomed place on the salon table, and the hall grew quiet again.

By all accounts, no one has dared to move it since.

The Vanished Bride

In another stately English home, another young woman haunted the corridors and bedchambers. The house was Marwell Hall, near Owlesbury in Hampshire, and the ghost was that of a lovely young bride. Years before, on her wedding day, she had enticed her guests into a game of hide-and-seek. Full of wine and high spirits, they had run wild about the house and grounds, secreting themselves in all sorts of out-of-the-way places. Hours later, when the game was done, everyone had been found but the bride herself.

A concerted search was mounted, but the house was huge and rambling, the grounds were extensive, and after hours of looking she had still not been discovered. No one knew quite what to do. The guests quietly left for their own homes, the groom wept for his lost bride, and the house was closed up for the night.

Her death only became apparent on subsequent nights, when her ghost — still in her wedding gown — began to roam the corridors at night, fumbling at locks, rustling bed curtains, playing perhaps at hide-and-seek. For years, the ghostly presence haunted the house, until a maid ventured one day into one of the dusty attics of the house. There she saw an oaken chest, firmly locked, and wondered what was inside. After something of a struggle, she pried it open, and stepped back in shock. Inside it lay a skeleton, still wrapped in wedding clothes. The bride, it seems, had been too good at the game; she had hidden herself in a chest that had accidentally closed — and latched. Her remains discovered and her fate made known, the bride of Marwell Hall was released from her earthly bondage. From that day forward, she haunted the house no more.

THE TOWER

𝒥f ever there was a place that begged to be haunted, that place must surely be the Tower of London — the stone fortress, rising above the river Thames, where the English monarchy has for centuries imprisoned and executed its real, and perceived, enemies.

Many ghosts, indeed, are said to wander its halls.

Lady Jane Grey is one; sometimes called the Nine Days' Queen, she was only seventeen in 1554 when she was imprisoned and beheaded on the Tower green.

Sir Walter Raleigh is another — he lived there for thirteen years, before James I, convinced he was plotting against the Throne, sent him, too, to the block in 1618.

The two Plantagenet princes, Edward and Richard, had many times been seen wandering the corridors, hand in hand. It was long thought that their uncle, later Richard III, had had them murdered there in 1483. But it wasn't until the seventeenth century that the skeletons of two small boys were unearthed near the Bloody Tower. Once their bones had been interred in Westminster Abbey, the spirits of the young princes disappeared.

Perhaps the most famous ghost to haunt the Tower of London is that of Anne Boleyn. Second wife of Henry VIII and mother of Elizabeth I, she

ns charged with adultery and incest (though in all probability her only
ue crime was that Henry had grown bored with her) and sentenced to
be executed. On the bright morning of May 19, 1536, she dressed in a
damask gown, a red petticoat, and a pearl headdress. (Surprised at her
spritely demeanor, the Governor of the Tower declared, "This lady has
much joy and pleasure in death.") And because, as she said, she had "a
little, little neck," she was granted a special favor: instead of being decap-
itated by a clumsy Englishman with an axe, she was provided with a
skilled Frenchman, able to do the job with a sword. When he'd finished,
the headless body was stuffed into an arrow case and buried under the
stones of the Tower chapel, St. Peter ad Vincula.

But it did not rest there. Many times she was seen where the block
had once stood, or roaming the grounds of the Tower keep. One sentry
reportedly died of fright; another fainted when the headless ghost
approached, then walked right through him. In the 1800s, an officer of
the guard took notice of a strange, soft, and unaccountable light filling
the windows of the locked chapel. When he put a ladder up to the window to peer inside, he nearly fell from his perch in terror.

Inside, he saw what looked like a gathering at a Tudor court —
ladies and gentlemen, all dressed in shimmering silks and glittering
jewels, parading through the candlelit chamber. As they made their
way in stately procession toward the altarpiece, each one seemed to
suddenly dissolve, as if drawn down again beneath the stones of the

floor. Among them he recognized, from her portraits, Queen Anne herself. When the last spectral figure had vanished, the light, too, was extinguished.

A short time later, the floor of the chapel was excavated, and the bones of Anne Boleyn and over two hundred other skeletons —the entire ghostly company — were found resting there.

SPECTRES OF THE SEA

*I*f sailors are the most superstitious folk on Earth, there is good reason for it. Any voyage they take may prove to be their last. Far from land, adrift on waters many fathoms deep, at the mercy of the elements, they must rely upon themselves, their fellows, and above all luck, if they hope ever to see their home port again.

Many sailors, of course, never do. Lost at sea, their ships sunk by raging storms, monstrous waves, or murderous broadsides, these unfortunates go, instead, to a place called Davy Jones's Locker. Ever since the eighteenth century, Davy Jones has been the sailors' common moniker for the evil spirit of the sea, and his locker — which sailors fervently pray they will never visit — is the ocean floor.

A sailor who dies happily, on the other hand, lying in his bed on dry land, goes to a heavenly spot known as Fiddler's Green; there, the fiddler always plays, the rum flows freely, and the women are forever willing.

Fire at sea, though a source of dread on most occasions, was in one instance an omen of good luck. Known as St. Elmo's fire, this was the bright, glowing light, created by electrical discharge, which sheathed the masts and yardarms of a ship after a storm. According to nautical lore, St. Elmo (the patron saint of Mediterranean seamen) died in a storm at sea, but not before promising the crewmen that if they were to survive the tempest themselves he would provide them with an unmistakable sign. The sailors waited anxiously, clinging to the railings, until they saw the ball of fire, and heard it crackling atop the mast. Then they knew that the worst of the storm had passed. (If, however, St. Elmo's fire descends to the deck itself, it is considered a bad omen; and if it glows around any particular sailor's head, that sailor should waste no time putting his earthly affairs in order.)

Then there were the so-called *fire-ships* — ghostly vessels that plied the seas, forever reliving their own destruction, or carrying souls to theirs. In Celtic legend, one such ship is sometimes seen off the Isle of Eigg, sailing past at an impossible speed, blazing with fire. On the deck a lean black creature dances about, laughing and sawing away at a fiddle as if at a country dance, while from below decks can be heard the pitiful cries of the damned being conveyed to Hell.

Another fire-ship, seen only once every seven years, is reputedly captained by the sea god Manannan himself. His galley is called *Wave Sweeper,* and he voyages from the Isle of Man to the Hebrides, gathering up the souls of all the good men who have died and transporting them into the western sea, where the Celtic paradise was thought to lie.

The spectre known as the "Palatine light" is one of the most tragic, and well documented, of these fiery phenomena. The actual *Palatine* was an 800-ton, Dutch-owned vessel, which had once been used for trading between France and Spain. But over the years it had become more and more decrepit, and by 1752, when it set out on its last disastrous voyage, sailors watching it being loaded said that they could smell the rot that was eating through its timbers.

What made this all the more horrifying was that its cargo was chiefly human — 304 emigrants, traveling from Amsterdam to the New World, to a city called Philadelphia.

The captain, a drunken lout, had already acquired an unsavory reputation. This 3000-mile voyage, which he had made before, was an arduous one, and due to the lack of facilities aboard and the ever-present threat of disease, there were always a certain number of fatalities. The captain had the privilege of first claim on the personal belongings of anyone who died, and it was rumored, as a consequence, that he had hurried several of these poor souls to their death.

For this particular voyage, the captain had hatched a truly diabolical plot. He had made arrangements to wreck the ship on the shores of Block Island, where a band of scavengers would be waiting to help salvage the cargo, and after stealing the emigrants' possessions, murder them. The proceeds were to be divvied up between the captain, his crew, and the Block Island scavengers.

But nineteen days out of Amsterdam, the captain's patience was wearing thin. The ship was making poor progress in heavy seas, and not enough of his passengers had already died of natural causes to keep him satisfied. So he decided to hasten things along by lining the emigrants up and robbing them at gunpoint. Anyone who protested was thrown overboard. The survivors were herded below deck again where they huddled for two more months until the coast of Rhode Island was at last seen.

At this point the records of the story become confused, but it appears that the crew mutinied, perhaps with an eye to keeping the captain's share, and killed him. Then they collected their loot, jumped into the lifeboats, and left the *Palatine* adrift.

The ship sailed on, unpiloted, until it crashed on the rocks of Block Island sometime between Christmas and New Year's Day. The scavengers were there, and they clambered aboard, stealing everything that was left and slaughtering any of the emigrants still alive. When they were done, they set fire to the ship and let the tide take the flaming wreck back out to sea. As they watched from the shore, they saw the figure of a woman, someone who had escaped their attention, racing back and forth across the blazing deck. From across the water, they could hear her shrieking in agony, screaming the name of her child, until the flames rose up around her.

By morning, the ship had disappeared completely.

Until one year later when the wraith of the *Palatine,* burning bright, was seen again just off the coast of Block Island, and the woman's screams were heard again above the crashing of the waves. Nor was that the last time the Palatine light cast its eerie glow; ever since, captains in their logs have reported sighting it in the waters off Rhode Island, burning from stem to stern, and drifting aimlessly into the night.

THE FLYING DUTCHMAN

There was one phantom that sailors feared above all others — a ghostly ship, with patched sails and a skeletal crew, it went by the name of the *Flying Dutchman*. Merely to catch sight of this ship was an ill omen for the sailors on any passing vessel.

Legend has it that the original captain was a blasphemous Dutchman who was sailing around the Cape of Good Hope when he encountered terrible headwinds that threatened to sink his ship and all aboard. The sailors warned him to turn around, the passengers pleaded, but the captain, either mad or drunk, refused to change course. Instead, he pressed on, singing loud and obscene songs, before going below to his cabin to drink beer and smoke his pipe. Monstrous waves pummeled the sides of the ship, howling winds bent the masts and tore at the sails, but still the captain held his course, challenging God Almighty to make him alter it.

Finally, there was a rebellion on board; the crew and passengers tried to take control of the ship, but the captain, roused from his drunken stupor, killed the leader of the mutiny and threw him over the side. The moment the body hit the water, the clouds parted, and a shadowy figure appeared on the quarterdeck.

"You're a very stubborn man," the shadow said, and the captain answered him with an oath.

"I never asked for a peaceful passage," the captain went on. "I never asked for anything. So clear off before I shoot you, too."

But the figure didn't move. Drawing his pistol, the captain tried to fire, but the gun exploded in his hand. Now the figure spoke again, and told the captain he was accursed. His fate was to sail the seas for eternity, never stopping for rest or anchorage, never finding a port, but always flying before the storm.

"Gall," the shadow said, "shall be your drink, and red hot iron your meat." Of his crew, only the cabin boy would accompany him, and "horns shall grow out of his forehead, and he shall have the muzzle of a tiger."

The captain, reckless to the last, cried, "Amen to that!"

And so, for centuries thereafter, the Flying Dutchman was seen piloting his ghostly vessel, its canvas spread, its masts creaking in a fearful wind. Sometimes, it was said, he led other ships astray, onto rocky shoals and hidden reefs. Sometimes he was said to be responsible for turning sailors' rations sour. His ship, looking innocent enough, would sometimes draw alongside another vessel and send letters aboard. But if the letters were opened and read, the ship would founder.

Those who saw the captain himself claimed that he was bareheaded and repentant, clutching the wheel on the quarterdeck, beseeching the heavens for mercy at last. In the rigging of his ship, some said, they could see a crew of skeletons, grinning merrily as they put on ever more sail.

Hell receiving its new tenants.

Glossary

A guide to terms, titles, and proper names included in the text.

Abbadon — demon, sovereign of the Bottomless Pit
Abduscius — demon who uproots trees
Abigor — demon cavalier, skilled in secrets of war
Acheron — a monster with flaming eyes who lives in Hell
Adramalech — demon, grand chancellor, supervisor of Satan's wardrobe
Agaliarept — demon who can discover all secrets
Aguares — demon, grand duke of Hell, inciter of dancing
Alastor — executor of court decrees in Hell
Amduscias — demon of disturbing music, a grand duke of Hell
Amon — a demon, marquis of Hell
Andras — a grand marquis of Hell
Ankou — a ghostly workman with a cart, who foretold death (Brittany)
Asmodeus — the demon of lust and marital discord

Astaroth — a demon, grand duke of Hell

Astarte — grand duke, and treasurer, of Hell

Athame — the ceremonial knife used by a witch

Azazel — standard bearer of the infernal legions

Baal — demon of guile and cunning, a grand duke of Hell

Baalberith — chief secretary of Hell

banshee — ghost of a washerwoman who foretold death (Ireland)

Barbatos — a demonic duke, able to reveal hidden treasure and knowledge of the past and future

Bathory, Elizabeth — a Carpathian countess executed in 1610 for bathing in young girls' blood

Beelzebub — Satan's second-in-command; aka Lord of the Flies

Behemoth — the huge demon who presides over feasting in Hell

Belial — a powerful ally of Satan, and demon of lies

Bellarmine Jug — aka witch bottle, used in casting a deadly spell

Belphegor — demon who seduced men with wealth

bier right — a trial ritual, used to determine a murderer's guilt

Bifrons — demon who moves bodies from one grave to another

Binsfeld, Peter — (c. 1540–1603) German authority on witchcraft

Black Book — a manual of magic, a grimoire

Black Shuck — a phantom hound that haunts the English countryside

Bodin, Jean — French lawyer and demonologist, author of *De La Demonomanie des Sorciers* (1580)

bokor — a Voodoo sorcerer

Book of Shadows — a witch's personal book of incantations, etc.

Bune — demon who, with Bifrons, moves bodies from their graves

bune wand — Scottish word for a witch's staff, or broomstick

Burton, Robert — (1577–1640) English clergyman and author

Cabala — originally of Jewish origin, a body of occult doctrine

Caim — demon who gives understanding of animals and nature

Cerridwen — Druidic moon goddess

changeling — a fairy child secretly switched with a human infant

cherubim — the second highest order of the Heavenly Host

Cocytus — a frozen marsh, the ninth circle of Hell

corpse candle — an eerie light, or *ignis fatuus* (Wales)

Dagon — demon, baker to Hell

Dantalian — demon who turns men's thoughts to evil

Dante Alighieri — (1265–1321) Italian poet, author of *The Divine Comedy*

Davy Jones's Locker — the bottom of the sea, where drowned sailors go

Del Rio, Martin Antoine — (1551–1608) Jesuit scholar, author of a handbook on witchcraft, *Disquisitionum Magicarum*

Dis — the poet Dante's name for Satan

doppelganger — "double goer" in German; a spirit double

dybbuk — in Jewish folklore, a wandering spirit

Elementals — the four elements — earth, air, fire, water — from which the universe was created

Esbat — the monthly meeting of a witches' coven, at the time of the full moon

fairies — a race of small, supernatural creatures

familiar — evil spirit, provided to do a witch's bidding

Faust — sixteenth-century magus who sold his soul to the devil

Fiddler's Green — the heavenly paradise of sailors

fire-ships — spectral vessels that sail the seas forever

Flauros — demon who, with Andras, commits murder

Fleurety — Beelzebub's lieutenant general, controls Africa

Flying Dutchman — a ghostly captain who pilots a ghostly ship for eternity

Forcas — grand president of Hell

Furfur — demon who controls thunder, lightning, strong winds

ghoul — an evil creature who robs graves and eats the dead

Gifford, George — English preacher, author of *Dialogue Concerning Witches* (1593)

Glasyalabolas — demon who incites men to murder

gnomes — the Elemental spirits of earth

goblins — mischievous and ugly fairies

golem — in Hebraic folklore, a monstrous man created by magic

Gomory — demon who procures love of women, especially girls

Gowdie, Isobel — Scottish witch in seventeenth century

grimoire — the magician's handbook of incantations, etc.

Guazzo, Francesco-Maria — Italian friar, author of *Compendium Maleficarum* (1608)

Haborym — demon of fire and holocaust

Halpas — demon who burned towns

Hand of Glory — a magical tool created from a hanged man's hand

homunculus — an artificial human created by alchemy

Hopkins, Matthew — (died 1647) self-appointed Witch-Finder General of England

houngan — a Voodoo priest

ignis fatuus — "foolish fire," a will-o'-the-wisp: eerie light, generally seen over swamps and in graveyards

imps — lowly demons, often kept by witches as their familiars

incubus — a male demon who preys upon women sexually

Josephus, Flavius — Jewish philosopher/naturalist, in first century A.D.

Key of Solomon — the most famous grimoire, attributed to King Solomon of Israel

Klein, Johann — law professor and specialist in sexual relations between witches and the devil, author of *Examen* (1731)

knockers — tiny spirits who worked in the mines of Cornwall

Kramer, Heinrich — fifteenth-century Dominican, coauthor of the *Malleus Maleficarum*

Lamia — female demon and vampire, who preys especially on children

Lemegeton — the Lesser Key of Solomon, a handbook of magic

Leonard — demon, master of the sabbats

Lerajie — demon, clad as archer, who incites battles

Lethe — the river of forgetfulness in Hell

Leviathan — the great serpent demon of Hell, ruler of the oceans

liekkio — "flaming one," the ghost of a child buried in the forest (Finland)

Lilin — the demon children of Lilith

Lilith — queen of the succubi, and Adam's first wife

limbo — the place where souls of virtuous pagans and unbaptized infants go

loa — in Voodoo religion, the spirits which inhabit the world

loubin — a haunter of cemeteries, or feeder on corpses (France)

loup-garou — a werewolf (France)

Lucifer — angel who rebelled against God, and fell from heaven; Satan

Lucifuge Rofocale — prime minister of Hell

lupin — a werewolf-like creature, which haunts graveyards

lycanthropy — the changing of men into werewolves

main-de-gloire — elf created from mandrake root (France)

Malebolge — the eighth ring of Hell, reserved for Fraudulence and Malice

Malebranche — the "evil clawed" demons in Dante's *Inferno*

maleficia — misfortune and injuries caused by witches

Malleus Maleficarum — *The Witches' Hammer* by Jakob Sprenger and Heinrich Kramer, a manual on witchcraft (1486)

Mammon — demon of riches and covetousness

mandrake — a plant thought to possess magical powers

Marbas — demon who can cause, or cure, disease

mare — aka nightmare, a demon that perches on the chest during sleep

Marlowe, Christopher — (1564–1593) English playwright, author of *The Tragical History of Doctor Faustus*

Melchom — demon, treasurer for princes in houses of Hell

Mephistopheles — demon who served Faust for twenty-four years

mermaids — half-woman, half-fish creatures who lived in the sea

mermen — the male equivalent of the mermaid

Milton, John — (1608–1674) English poet, author of *Paradise Lost*

Moloch — demon/deity, to whom children were sacrificed

Mulciber — demon, architect of buildings in Pandaemonium

Murmur — demon who takes charge of the soul

Murrell, James ("Cunning") — (1780–1860) English herbalist/seer

navky — spirits of murdered or unbaptized children (Slavic)

Nebiros — demon, field marshal in Hell

nixies — green-haired, malevolent water spirits (German)

Nybras — demon, in charge of pleasures in Hell

Nysrock — demon, chef in Hell

Oiellet — demon who tempts men, and monks in particular, to break their vow of poverty

Olivier — a fallen archangel who encourages cruelty toward the poor

osculum infame — the kiss of shame (witches kissed Satan's backside at the sabbat)

Pandaemonium — Satan's capital city in Hell

Paracelsus — (1493–1541) Swiss physician and alchemist

Paymon — demon, in charge of public ceremonies in Hell

pentacle — a five-pointed figure used as a symbol in magical rites

Petronius — author, in the first century A.D., of the *Satyricon*

Philosopher's Stone — the secret material sought by alchemists to convert base metals to gold

Philotanus — demon of sodomy and pederasty

Phlegethon — a river of boiling blood in Hell

Pliny — Greek naturalist, in first century A.D.

poltergeist — a "racketing ghost" (in German) who creates a commotion

Prelati, Francesco — Florentine priest, alchemist to Gilles de Rais

Procel — demon who makes water freezing cold or scalding hot

Psellus, Michaelis — (c. 1018–1080) Byzantine philosopher and statesman

psychopomp — a person, or sometimes a bird, sent to convey a spirit to the next world

Put Satanachia — commander-in-chief of Satan's army

Rais, Gilles de — (1404–1440) French lord and mass murderer

Raum — demon count, and destroyer of cities

relatio — the written record of a witch's trial and confession

sabbat — a gathering/feast of witches

Sabnack — demon who causes mortal bodies to decay

St. Elmo's fire — a bright glow on a ship's mast after a storm; a good omen to sailors

salamanders — the Elemental spirits of fire

Sargatanas — demon and brigadier major of Hell

Satan — the supreme lord of Hell and its demons

Scot, Reginald — (1538–1599) English author of *Discoverie of Witchcraft* (1584)

scrying — the practice of crystal-gazing to achieve clairvoyance

Seera — demon who makes time fly, or crawl

sendings — murderous ghosts, made from human bone (Iceland)

Seraphim — the highest order of the Heavenly Host

Shax — demon who blinds and deafens his victims

Simon Magus — sorcerer and founder of a gnostic sect in second century A.D.

Sinistrari, Ludovico Maria — (1622–1701) theologian, author of *De Daemonialitate*

Solomon — King of Israel in the tenth century B.C.

speculum — the crystal ball, or mirror, used by witches for purposes of divining

Spina, Alphonsus de — fifteenth-century Spanish theologian, author of *Fortalicium Fidei* (*Fortress of Faith*)

Sprenger, Jakob — fifteenth-century Dominican, coauthor of *Malleus Maleficarum*

Stoker, Bram — Irish author of *Dracula* (published in 1897)

succubus — a female demon who preys on men sexually

swimming the witch — a test in which a witch was ducked to see if she would sink or float

Sylphs (sylvestres) — the Elemental spirits of air

Sytry — demon who causes women to show themselves naked

transvection — the witch's ability to fly through the night air

undines — the Elemental spirits of water

Uphir — demon, physician in Hell to other demons

utburd — the ghost of a dead infant (Norway)

Valafar — demon who presides over robbers and brigands

vampire — a dead person who revives by drinking human blood

Verdelet — master of ceremonies in Hell

Vine — demon who tears down great walls, makes storms at sea

Voodoo — a polytheistic religion, practiced chiefly in the West Indies, mixing African cult worship with Catholic elements

warlock — a male witch

Watchers — an order of angels who lusted after, and corrupted, mortal women

Weird Sisters — the three witches who appear in *Macbeth*

werewolf — a human who has been transformed into a wolf

Wesley, Rev. Samuel — (1662–1735) English clergyman, host to the Epworth Poltergeist

West, William — English lawyer, author of *Simboleography* (1594)

Weyer, Johan — (1515–1588) German physician, author of *De Praestigiis,* which exposed the witchcraft delusion

witch—a man or woman using magic or occult powers to achieve their ends

witch ball — a speculum used by witches for divining

Witch's Ladder — a charm woven by witches to do harm to an enemy

witch's mark — the supernumerary nipple or other spot where a witch suckled her familiar

Xaphan — demon who stoked the fires of Hell

Zepar — demon who drove women to madness

zombie — a corpse reanimated by a bokor, made to do his will

Zosimus – a Greek philosopher and alchemist of the third or fourth century A.D.

BIBLIOGRAPHY

Alexander, Peter, ed. *The Complete Works of Shakespeare*. London and Glasgow: William Collins Sons & Co., Ltd., 1958.

Ausubel, Nathan, ed. *A Treasury of Jewish Humor*. New York: M. Evans and Company, 1951.

Barber, Paul. *Vampires, Burial, and Death*. New Haven: Yale University Press, 1988.

Baskin, Wade. *Dictionary of Satanism*. New York: Philosophical Library, 1972.

Beck, Emily Morison, ed. *Familiar Quotations by John Bartlett*, Fourteenth Edition. Boston: Little, Brown and Company, 1968.

Brown, Raymond Lamont. *Phantoms of the Sea*. London: Patrick Stephens Limited, 1972.

Cavendish, Richard, ed. *Encyclopedia of the Unexplained*. London: Routledge & Kegan Paul, 1974.

Cavendish, Richard, ed. *Man, Myth and Magic: An Illustrated Encyclopedia of the Supernatural*. New York: Marshall Cavendish Corporation, 1970.

Chaplin, J.P. *Dictionary of the Occult and Paranormal*. New York: Laurel/Dell Publishing, 1976.

Cuddon, A.J., ed. *The Penguin Book of Ghost Stories*. New York: Viking Penguin, 1984.

Dante Alighieri. *The Divine Comedy*. The Carlyle-Wicksteed translation. New York: Random House, 1950.

Daraul, Arkon. *Witches and Sorcerers*. London: Frederick Muller, Ltd., 1962.

Davidson, Gustav. *A Dictionary of Angels.* New York: The Free Press, 1967.

Davis, Wade. *The Serpent and the Rainbow*. New York: Warner Books, 1985.

Day, Harvey. *Occult Illustrated Dictionary*. London: Kaye and Ward, 1975.

Drury, Nevill. *Dictionary of Mysticism and the Occult*. San Francisco: Harper and Row, 1985.

Edwards, Gillian. *Hobgoblin and Sweet Puck*. London: Geoffrey Bles, 1974.

Frazer, Sir James George. *The Golden Bough*. New York: Macmillan Publishing Co., 1922.

Gettings, Fred. *Dictionary of Demons*. North Pomfret, Vermont: Trafalgar Square Publishing, 1980.

Godwin, Malcolm. *Angels—An Endangered Species*. New York: Simon and Schuster, 1990.

Grant, Michael and John Hazel. *Who's Who in Classical Mythology*. New York: Oxford University Press, 1993.

Gupta, Marie, and Fran Brandon. *A Treasury of Witchcraft and Devilry*. Middle Village, New York: Jonathan David Publishers, 1975.

Hallam, Jack. *Ghosts' Who's Who*. North Pomfret, Vermont: David and Charles, 1977.

Hill, Douglas, and Pat Williams. *The Supernatural*. London: Aldus Books, 1965.

Kendrick, Walter. *The Thrill of Fear*. New York: Grove Weidenfeld, 1991.

Kerenyi, C. *The Gods of the Greeks*. London: Thames and Hudson, 1982.

Maple, Eric. *The Dark World of Witches*. London: Robert Hale Limited, 1962.

Marsden, Simon. *Phantoms of the Isles*. Exeter, England: Webb and Bower, 1990.

Milton, John. *Complete Poetry and Selected Prose of John Milton*. New York: Random House, 1942.

Murray, Margaret. *The God of the Witches*. London: Sampson Low, Marston & Co., Ltd., 1933.

O'Donnell, Elliott. *Haunted Britain*. London: Rider and Company, 1956.

Otten, Charlotte F., ed. *A Lycanthropy Reader: Werewolves in Western Culture*. Syracuse, New York.: Syracuse University Press, 1986.

Phillips, Ellen, ed. *The Enchanted World: Ghosts*. New York: Time-Life Books, Inc., 1984.

Robbins, Russell Hope. *The Encyclopedia of Witchcraft and Demonology*. New York: Crown Publishers, 1959.

Ronay, Gabriel. *The Truth About Dracula*. New York: Stein and Day, 1972.

St. Leger-Gordon, Ruth. *The Witchcraft and Folklore of Dartmoor*. London: Robert Hale, 1965.

Spence, Lewis. *The Fairy Tradition in Britain*. London: Rider and Company, 1948.

Sullivan, Jack, ed. *The Penguin Encyclopedia of Horror and the Supernatural*. New York: Viking, 1986.

Sullivan, J.P., trans. *Petronius: The Satyricon and the Fragments*. Baltimore, Maryland: Penguin Books, 1965.

Summers, Montague, ed. *Compendium Maleficarum of Brother Francesco Maria Guazzo*. London: John Rodker, 1929.

Summers, Montague. *The Geography of Witchcraft*. Evanston, Illinois: University Books, 1958.

Summers, Montague. *A Popular History of Witchcraft*. New York: Dutton, 1937.

Turner, Alice K. *The History of Hell*. New York: Harcourt Brace and Company, 1993.

Valiente, Doreen. *An ABC of Witchcraft Past and Present*. New York: St. Martin's Press, 1973.

Waite, Arthur Edward. *The Book of Black Magic and Ceremonial Magic*. New York: Causeway Books, 1973.

Wilde, Lady. *Ancient Legends, Mystic Charms and Superstitions of Ireland*. London: Chatto and Windus, 1902.

Williams, Charles. *Witchcraft*. London: Faber and Faber Limited, 1941.

Wilson, Colin. *The Supernatural: Mysterious Powers*. London: Aldus Books, 1975.

Wilson, Colin, and John Grant, eds. *The Directory of Possibilities*. Exeter, England: Webb and Bower, 1981.

Wolf, Leonard. *A Dream of Dracula*. Boston: Little, Brown and Company, 1972.

Wolf, Leonard. *The Essential Dracula*. New York: Plume, 1993.

Wright, Dudley. *The Book of Vampires*. Detroit: Omnigraphics, Inc., 1989.

ILLUSTRATION CREDITS

ABOUT THE AUTHOR

An author and journalist living in Los Angeles, Robert Masello has written articles and essays for some of the most prominent national publications, including *New York* magazine, *The Washington Post, New York Newsday,* and *The Los Angeles Times.* Among his many books, published both here and abroad, are three novels of the occult — *The Spirit Wood, Black Horizon,* and *Private Demons.*